MAKING MAJOR SALES

Making Major Sales

Neil Rackham

Gower

Published by
Gower Publishing Company Limited,
Gower House,
Croft Road,
Aldershot,
Hants GU11 3HR,
England

British Library Cataloguing in Publication Data

Rackham, Neil
    Making major sales.
    1. Selling
    I. Title
    658.8'5   HF5438.25

ISBN 0-566-02627-9

Reprinted 1987, 1988, 1990, 1991

Printed in Great Britain by Galliard (Printers) Ltd, Great Yarmouth

Contents

Illustrations

Preface

This is yet another book about how to sell more successfully. So what makes it different from the more than 1000 sales books which have already been published? Two things:

- *It's about the larger sale*
  Almost all existing books on selling have used models and methods which were developed in low-value, one-call sales. In the 1920s, E.K. Strong carried out pioneering studies of small sales which introduced such new ideas to selling as features and benefits, closing techniques, objection handling methods and open and closed questions. For more than sixty years those same concepts have been copied, adapted and refined with the assumption that they should apply to *all* sales. Even the few writers who have tried to give some advice on larger sales have based many of their ideas on these older models. And that's a mistake, because the traditional selling strategies just don't work in the fast-moving and complex environment of today's major sale. This, I believe, is the first book to take a completely fresh look at larger sales and the skills you need to make them succeed. As you will find, many of the things which help you in smaller sales will hurt your success as the sale grows larger. Major sales demand a new and different set of skills, and that's what this book is about.
- *It's based on research*
  This is the first publication of results for the largest research project ever undertaken in the selling skills area. My team at Huthwaite analysed more than 35 000 sales calls, over a period of twelve years, to provide the hard facts on successful selling which you'll read here. There are plenty of *opinions* on how to sell, but a real shortage of well-researched facts. We carried out the research described in this book because I wasn't satisfied with opinions. I wanted *proof*. And now, as a result of our research, I can give you well-documented evidence about how to be more successful in larger sales.

I'm writing for those who are serious about selling, who see their selling as a high-level profession which needs all the skill and care which goes with professionalism in any field. And I'm writing about how to make major sales – significant business which has the margins and rewards which are attractive for high-level sales professionals. In our studies we've worked with top salespeople from over twenty of the world's sales organisations. From watching them in action during major sales, we've been able to find out what makes them so successful. That's the subject of this book.

But how do you know that the methods I'll be describing can help *you* to be more effective? I'm confident that they will. And my confidence is based on something more substantial than just hope. When we first discovered the methods described in this book, we weren't sure whether they would help people to sell more effectively. For one thing, many of our findings were controversial and directly contradicted most existing sales training; for another, we weren't sure whether the methods used by successful professionals would be too difficult for most people to learn.

So we kept quiet about our findings for seven years, testing out the practical value of our ideas before we were ready to publish them. During that time we trained several thousand salespeople in the methods we describe here, continuously experimenting to find the best way to turn our theoretical knowledge of sales success into simple and practical methods which anyone could use to help them become more effective in major sales. We measured the productivity gain of the first thousand people we trained, comparing them with control groups from the same companies. The people we'd trained showed an average increase in sales volume of 17 per cent more than the control groups. Consequently, I'm confident that the advice in this book is a well-tested method for increasing sales results. It's already helped thousands of people be more successful in larger sales – and it can give the same help to you.

I once read a preface which said, 'I've nobody to thank except you, the reader, who has shelled out money for my book'. What a splendidly self-contained author! I'm at the other extreme – my thank-you list runs into thousands. First and foremost, there are the more than 10 000 salespeople in twenty-three countries who generously agreed to let Huthwaite researchers travel with them and observe them in action during sales calls. Then there are upwards of 1000 sales managers who have been part of programmes we've run across the world and who have helped collect data and refine the ideas I'm presenting here.

Finally, at last count, there were more than 100 people who were closely involved in the research itself and in the development of our ideas. I can't include them all, but special mention must go to Peter Honey, Rose Evison and Terry Morgan, who worked with us to develop the original behaviour analysis methodology we used in our research. From that methodological base, we were able to produce some initial measurement instruments which let us take the first ever scientific, quantitative look at sales calls. Roger Sugden deserves special mention as the first member of the Huthwaite research team to use these early methods.

For the development of the SPIN® model itself, much of the credit should go to Linda Marsh and Simon Bailey. They've influenced every part of the research; they carried out the initial field studies to validate the model and their expertise and good judgement has guided all subsequent developments. Many other Huthwaite colleagues have contributed, including Joan Costich, who helped me revise the manuscript, and Elaine Ailsworth, who prepared the illustrations.

People outside Huthwaite who have made substantial contributions include Masaaki Imai of the Cambridge Corporation, who has adapted our models to fit the fascinating Japanese sales environment; Jan van den Berg of McKinsey and Co, who has forced me to express these concepts in fewer words than I thought decent; and Malcolm Stern of Gower, who suggested many useful changes to improve the book's clarity.

Neil Rackham

1

The Huthwaite research

It was a miserable January evening. I'd been working with my first important client and, after a hard week, I was anxious to get home. Boarding the train, my head full of the week's events, I scarcely noticed the only other passenger in the compartment. But three hours later, when we were halted by freezing fog, the stranger and I got into one of those soul-baring conversations which happen between stranded travellers. I explained that I'd recently left a university research fellowship in order to found my own research consultancy. 'How is it going?' he asked. 'Much tougher than I'd expected', I confessed. 'The trouble with research is that it's much harder to sell than something tangible like a product.' 'I'm in selling', he told me. 'Like you, I've just changed jobs and I'm finding it hard. I used to be a top performer for my last company, but now . . . well, I just can't seem to do anything right.'

A few questions revealed that my unhappy travelling companion had previously been selling low-priced products. Out of a sales force of two hundred, he had been number three in terms of sales volume. Feeling himself ready for bigger things, he moved to a new company where he was selling expensive machine tools. He'd been there a year and was in real trouble. 'It's like day and night', he complained. 'Instead of being in the top three, I'm now right at the bottom – and I don't know what's gone wrong. How can you be successful in one sales job and fail entirely in another?'

I had no answers, except for all the usual platitudes about everybody going through a bad patch from time to time. At the next station I watched him leave – a Victorian image of a hunched-up figure trudging gloomily into the swirling fog. For the rest of the journey I thought about his problem. As I'd told him, there was almost no hard research into sales success, certainly nothing which would help explain why somebody could be outstanding in one type of sale and an abject failure in another.

At the time I was even more puzzled than he was. And as a research psychologist I hated to be puzzled. He had asked me a practical question about human behaviour which I couldn't even begin to answer. I've been thinking about this question ever since.

Perhaps that journey was the genesis of the Huthwaite Research Group studies of effective selling. Since that conversation, my colleagues and I have spent 12 years analysing over 35 000 sales transactions. We've studied 116 factors which might play some part in sales performance and we've researched effective selling in 23 countries. Our studies constitute the largest ever investigation into sales success. Now, with the benefit of a million dollars of systematic research, we could give my fellow traveller the answers he was looking for. We could tell him, for example, that:

1

- many of the skills which helped make him successful in smaller sales were actually *preventing* his success with larger sales
- major sales, which require a number of calls to take the business, demand an entirely different selling style from the one-call sale
- customer behaviour changes significantly as the size of sale grows, and demands a different set of skills from the seller.

And, as you'll find in this book, there's a whole lot more we could tell him which would explain why he was having difficulties and, more importantly, exactly what he could do to increase his sales successes.

Our first mistake

Generals write about victories, doctors about recoveries and researchers about successful projects. We all bury our failures. In the early stages of our project we made a string of expensive mistakes. Most of them I can now mercifully ignore, but there's one which deserves closer examination. Put yourself in my shoes. Here I was, ready to study effective selling. I'd been able to persuade a number of multinational clients that they needed to know more about what made for success in the larger sale. I had the budget, but how was I going to spend it? In my place, how would *you* have started an investigation of success in the major sale?

Possibly you would have done as we did; you would have found some top salespeople and interviewed them to discover the secrets of their success. And you would have found, as we found, that top performers rarely know what it is which makes them more effective. That's not only true in selling: it's true of top performers in every field. Very few top

athletes ever become top coaches, for exactly the same reason. Good performers often do things naturally without even realising what it is that makes them different. The points which they try to pass on to others are usually those little extras they've had to work on – not the mainstream things they do without thinking.

I raise this point for two reasons. Firstly, it set our research back by at least a year and even today many researchers are wasting precious resources trying unsuccessfully to understand skills using interview methods. But the second reason is more important. How have *you* learned how to sell? Most of us learn partly by our own trial and error, partly by taking advice from those we regard as good performers. And that's the problem. How useful is the advice we're given? In our experience it pays to be very cautious about advice from experts, whether it's another book by 'the world's greatest salesman' or a top seller talking at a sales conference.

Let's start this book with some frank advice. Don't trust what top performers tell you. All our research experience indicates that there's a great difference between what effective salespeople say they do and what we've actually observed from going out with them. If you want to find out how experts sell, then travel with them and watch them in action, don't rely on what they tell you afterwards.

Don't trust experts: a case study

Looking back on all those wasted interviews, I now realise that I should have known better. A few years earlier I'd done some research into catching smugglers which showed clearly just how unreliable, 'Here's how I do it . . .' advice can be. My company, Huthwaite Research Group, had been asked by a couple of government agencies to do a study to find out why some customs officers had a much higher hit rate than others. We found 23 customs agents who each had a consistent and outstanding record in stopping and detecting smugglers. We interviewed all 23 in an attempt to discover the secret of their success. Eighteen out of the 23 told us the same story. 'It's all in the eyes', they explained, 'look into people's eyes and you can see signs of guilt'. We were unsuspecting enough to believe them, and even set up some training for less-successful customs officers which involved people gazing earnestly into each others' eyes. It created a lot of embarrassment but, so far as I know, didn't contribute anything to catching smugglers. After a while we changed our method. Instead of interviews we took to watching successful customs officers at work, using concealed cameras. Our studies revealed that successful customs officers were picking out signs of *control*, not of guilt. Even the proverbially innocent old lady looks guilty as anything under the scrutiny of a customs official. The truly guilty betray themselves by a number of signs such as a more upright posture and tighter neck muscles. Those were the signs of control which the successful agents were picking out. Despite the interview testimony of 18 out of 23 officers, it was nothing to do with guilt or eyes.

At the time when we were starting out on our sales research, the BBC produced a series called *The Experimenters*. It was about people who took an unusual approach to scientific investigation and the first programme was based on the work which we had done to establish better methods for detecting smugglers. During the filming I was discussing our research on camera. 'Remember,' I said confidently, 'if you want to learn what makes people skilled at a job, then watch them in action, *don't* try to learn from discussions and interviews.' Afterwards, while I was watching the playbacks, the dreadful realisation hit me that, in our studies of selling, we were violating this principle. We had been using interview

and questionnaire methods. No wonder we were finding nothing useful. Don't fall victim to our mistake. Never trust high performers to describe skills.

Studying sales performance

If you can't learn from interviewing top performers, what other methods are open to you? It's fine to say, 'Go out and watch people at work', but that's much harder than it sounds. What should you be looking for when you watch a top seller in action? How can you compare one sales call with another? How can you remain objective? What sort of measurement methods can you use? In Huthwaite Research Group we had pioneered a method called *behaviour analysis*. (For those interested in the intricate details, I've written a number of specialist books on the method, culminating in *Behaviour Analysis in Training*, McGraw-Hill, 1977.)

Put briefly, the behaviour analysis method works as in Figure 1.1.

1 *Choose your behaviour*
    Select some aspect of sales behaviour which you think might tie in with success. You might, for example, hold the theory that success in selling can be increased by frequently beating your fist on the customer's desk.

2 *Watch sales calls, counting how often the key behaviour occurs*
    Go with salespeople into actual calls and observe how often they beat their fists on the desk. Take a frequency count, so that you can say afterwards, 'In this call there were 11 examples of fist-beating, while in that call there were 17'.

3 *Divide calls into those which succeeded and those which failed*
    This step is harder than it sounds. What's the definition of a successful call? We'll come back to this point in more detail later, but for now let's

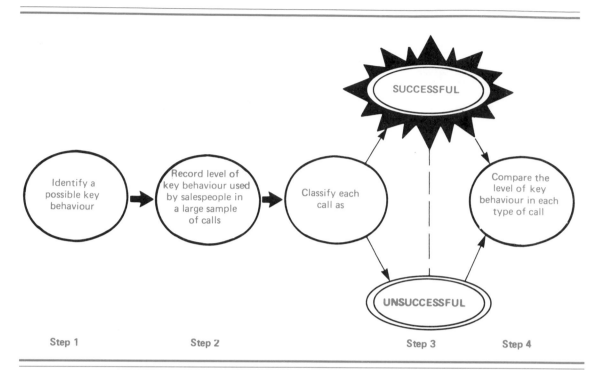

Figure 1.1   Analysing successful sales behaviour

assume that it's a call which either results in an order or makes some positive move towards getting the business. Divide all the calls where you've been observing fist-beating into two piles. In one pile put all the successful calls, in the other put the calls which failed.

4   *Analyse frequency differences*
Compare the average number of fist-beating in successful calls with the number of calls which failed. If fist-beating is a behaviour positively related to sales effectiveness, you should find more of it in the successful calls. If the average level of fist-beating is about the same in both successful and unsuccessful calls, then you can assume that it's not related to success – in other words, it doesn't make any difference to sales effectiveness one way or the other. Finally, if fist-beating is much higher in the calls which failed, then it's likely that

there's a negative relationship to success – the more fist-beating, the less likely the call will be to succeed.

Of course, as a researcher, I can't help pointing out that it's not quite this simple. You have to have objective methods and precise definitions to carry out studies of this kind. Even in this case, your researchers would have to have a standardised definition of fist-beating. They would have to agree, for example, whether drumming the fingers on a customer's desk should be included, or whether it would still be fist-beating if the seller beat a chair instead of the desk. They would need to observe large numbers of calls to collect statistically valid samples and to control for other variables. To draw conclusions, even about something as simple as beating your fist on a customer's desk, might take a month of observation, involve over a hundred calls and cost upwards of $10 000!

Despite the many advantages of the behaviour analysis method, its high cost has prevented it from being used more widely by researchers, who can't usually raise the large budgets required. It's only when an independent research corporation like Huthwaite can attract substantial funding from large clients that behaviour analysis-based research becomes possible. This book is the first publication of research which took us many years to complete. Before writing about our findings, my Huthwaite colleagues Simon Bailey, Linda Marsh and Bernard Midgley spent several years carefully testing out our conclusions in some of the world's leading sales companies. In the chapters which follow, you'll learn some surprising things. For example:

- *Closing techniques*
  The closing techniques which work in smaller accounts will actually *lose* you business as the sale grows larger. Most commonly taught closing techniques just don't work, so instead I'll be describing better ways of obtaining customer commitment in the major sale.

- *Probing methods*
  The classic questioning methods of open and closed questions may work in small sales but they certainly won't help you in bigger ones. I'll introduce you to the SPIN ® method of probing, which we discovered from the analysis of several thousand successful sales calls and from watching some of the world's top salespeople in action.

- *Objection handling*
  In major sales, objection-handling skills will contribute very little to your sales effectiveness. Successful sellers concentrate on objection-prevention, not on objection-handling. We've analysed how they do it and I'll be describing ways in which you can cut the number of objections you get from your customers by more than half.

- *New types of benefits*
  Since the 1920s we've been taught that a benefit shows how a feature can be used or can help the customer. This type of benefit can be very successful in the small scale. In the large one it fails entirely. I'll be introducing a new type of benefit which *is* successful in large sales.

You may not agree with everything I say. I'm used to that. I was once pulled off a stage in Los Angeles by an angry sales trainer for showing that his favourite closing technique was losing him sales. But this book isn't Neil Rackham's personal opinion of how to succeed in the major sale. It's a painstaking analysis of the success of many thousands of salespeople – collected from the most extensive research ever carried out in major account selling.

You'll find that I draw illustrations from small sales as well as from large. Sometimes I'll do this specifically to show how larger sales are different – sometimes just because examples from smaller sales can illustrate a point more simply. I'll also be drawing cases from a wide variety of selling situations. The sales calls we've studied come from more than fifty industries, and represent many hundreds of diverse products and services. In researching this diversity, the common factor in our studies has been the analysis of *success*. What are the skills which make one call more successful than another, whether you're selling professional services, capital goods or complex systems? That's the question I'll be setting out to answer for you in future chapters.

2

Sales large and small

There's been more written about the definition of major sales than about how to sell successfully once you've defined them. I'm not going to bore you with definitions. I'm sure that whatever term you use for them – whether you talk of major account sales, big ticket sales, system sales, large accounts, bulk sales, or just 'the big ones' – you know a major sale when you meet one.

What I *shall* do is briefly run through some of the characteristics of major sales in terms of customer psychology. It's changes in customer perceptions and behaviour that make major sales different. Let's look at what some of those differences are and how they can affect your selling.

Length of selling cycle

The simple low-value sale can often be completed in one call – a major sale may require many calls spread over a period of months. One of my former classmates selling in the aircraft industry once spent three years without making a single sale. On the face of it it sounds as if I'm just making the obvious point that major sales take longer. But that's not it. What's really important is that multi-call sales have a completely different psychology from single-call sales. For example, in a single-call sale the buying decision is usually taken then and there with the

seller present. In a multi-call sale the most important discussions and deliberations go on when the seller *isn't* present, during the interval between calls. Just suppose I'm a brilliant orator who can give a truly compelling product pitch. I'm likely to do well in the single call sale. That's because the person I'm selling to can be sufficiently impressed by the excellence of my pitch to say 'yes' on the spot and give me an order.

But what happens if it's a longer selling cycle, so that I don't take the order immediately after I've made my pitch? How much of what I've said will the customer remember tomorrow after I've gone? Could the customer repeat my smoothly polished presentation to her boss? Questions like these prompted us to do a small study in an office products company. The company had prepared a 'canned' script to demonstrate the eight most important advantages of their new wordprocessor. The script had been written by top professional advertising people and it was good. During initial testing the company was delighted. Pilot groups of customers rated the demonstration script very highly. The company's marketing executives anticipated that there would be an overall increase in business from customers who had attended the scripted demonstrations.

Unfortunately, very little of the anticipated business materialised. We were employed to find out why. So we asked a group of potential customers to sit

During the presentation the seller makes 8 key points

Immediately after the presentation potential customers can remember an average of 5.7 points

... but one week later, more than half has been forgotten: only 2.5 points remain

Figure 2.1   How much of a sales presentation do potential customers remember?

through the demonstration and to answer some questions immediately afterwards. As you can see, the script seemed to be quite effective. On average 5.7 of the 8 key points were remembered. But, a week later, when we visited each potential customer and tested their recall, we found that more than half had been forgotten (Figure 2.1).

What's worse, immediately after the presentation, customers gave high ratings for their probability of buying the product. However, just a week later, the average rating from those same customers indicated that they were now *unlikely* to buy (Figure 2.2).

What does this mean, and what's it got to do with one-call sales? From these studies, I'd draw the conclusion that a very good product pitch can have a *temporary* effect on a customer, but a week later it's largely gone. So, if you can get a decision

on the spot – as you usually can in a one-call sale – then there's no reason why you shouldn't use the temporary effect of a product pitch to raise customer enthusiasm and help you get the business immediately. But woe betide you if you can't get an instant decision. By next week your customers will have forgotten most of what you've said and will have lost their enthusiasm for your product.

Another of our findings, which we'll examine in much more detail later, was that in the one-call sale you could sell by pushing the benefits of your product, overcoming any objections and closing hard for the business. But, in a multi-call sale, that style was usually dangerously unsuccessful. Why? Perhaps your own experience as a buyer gives the answer. I can remember, for example, going into a car showroom a few months ago. The seller was one of those pushy types who over-populate the motor trade. After a

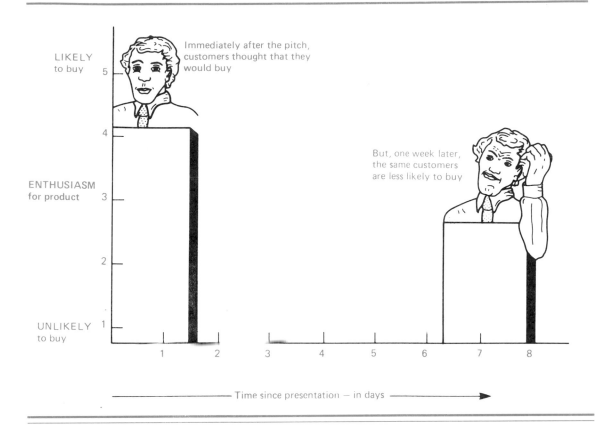

LIKELY
to buy

ENTHUSIASM
for product

UNLIKELY
to buy

Immediately after the pitch, customers thought that they would buy

But, one week later, the same customers are less likely to buy

Time since presentation — in days

Figure 2.2   Changes in customer enthusiasm for a product

couple of perfunctory questions, he gave me a really hard sell, using all the classic closes in the book. I wasn't ready to decide, so his pressure was both unwelcome and irritating. After I finally escaped, I made all sorts of solemn vows never to return to that showroom. I'm sure you've had the same kind of experience. Few customers will elect to go back for a repeat dose of pressure. In terms of your own selling, if you pressure a potential customer, then they won't want to meet you again. The rule seems to be that it's okay to be pushy if you can take the order there and then, but once you and your customer part company without an order, your pushiness has *reduced* your chance of final success. And, because the customer doesn't want to talk to you again, you may never discover where you went wrong. So, while a pushy or hard-

sell style may work in smaller sales, it generally acts against you when several calls are needed to take the business.

Size of customer's commitment

Almost by definition, large purchases involve bigger decisions from the customer and this alters the psychology of the sale. In a small sale the customer is less conscious of *value*. As the size of the sale increases, successful salespeople must build up the perceived value of their products or services. The building of perceived value is probably the single most important selling skill in larger sales. We've studied it in detail and several chapters of the book are devoted

9

to how to increase the value of what you offer your customers.

Several years ago we started a study which, because of a reorganisation in our client's salesforce, was never completed. That's a pity, because it was all about how the need to sell value increases as the sale gets larger. The client, who sold high-cost products, had asked us to advise on whether it was possible to recruit new salespeople whose only previous selling experience had been with cheaper goods. At the point where the project was stopped we were coming up with some interesting answers. We found that the salespeople who didn't successfully transfer to handling larger sales were those who had difficulty building the customer's perception of value.

I remember meeting one of these less-succesful people at Buffalo airport, prior to going out with him to make some calls. He was sitting on a bench with his briefcase open and surrounded by enough product literature to keep a paper recycling factory in business for months. He explained, miserably, that he was learning product details because he thought it would help him be more successful. 'In my last job', he explained, 'I was selling consumer goods and it was my product knowledge which made all the difference.' He may have been right, but it was his product knowledge which *prevented* him from being successful an hour later as I watched him fail to convince an office manager to buy a large copying system. The customer was understandably nervous at the thought of spending tens of thousands of dollars. The seller tried to cope with this uncertainty by talking in detail about the product, displaying all his newly acquired product knowledge. It didn't work. The reason why the customer wouldn't buy was that she didn't see enough *value* to justify so large a decision. After all, her present copier worked relatively well. It was true that there were some reliability problems and that copy quality wasn't

great, but did that justify spending a five-figure sum to put right? Not on your life – and all the seller's carefully memorised product knowledge couldn't alter the basic fact that his customer didn't perceive value. How should he have handled the call? Later chapters on the SPIN® method will show in detail how to build increased value in cases such as this. But the message to take now from the call in Buffalo is that what may work well in the smaller sale can act against you in the large ones.

The ongoing relationship

Most major sales involve an ongoing relationship with the customer. Partly that's because large purchases usually require some post-sales support – which means that buyer and seller must meet one or more times after the sale. Also, those people selling major goods or services usually generate most of their business from developing their existing customers. In contrast a smaller sale may often be a one-off event where the buyer will never meet the seller again.

How does this affect customer decision psychology? Perhaps the easiest way to illustrate it is through a personal example. Nowadays, as Chairman of the company, I'm more often doing the buying than the selling. A few weeks ago, as a buyer, I had the perfect illustration of how the ongoing relationship of a large sale can influence decisions. I was involved in two sales on the same day. The first sale was a small one. I needed a new overhead projector for my office, so I had asked a local supplier to send a sales rep to talk to me. The character who appeared was a remarkably unlovely individual who wouldn't have been out of place selling pornography in the back streets of Rio. 'It's your lucky day,' he began, 'I'm sure you can't wait to hear the deal I've got for you!' Actually, what I couldn't wait to do was to get him out of my office. But his price was good, I needed a projector and I'd never have to see him again. So I cut short his sales pitch, gave him the order and sent him on his way in five minutes flat. From his point of view, it was a successful sale. In most senses it was also successful for me as a buyer. I'd got a new projector at a good price – and all it took was five sleazy minutes.

Later that day I was involved in a much more significant sale. We were thinking of changing both the hardware and the software of our accounting system. The change would mean a couple of new computers, an integrated suite of accounting software and six months of time to put the whole thing together. I estimated we were talking about at least a $70 000 decision. The seller was a reasonable enough person – perhaps a little shallow and maybe just a bit *too* anxious to do business – but certainly a great improvement on the overhead projector rep I had bought from earlier in the day. Nevertheless, as the sales call progressed, I found myself becoming hesitant. As in the overhead projector sale, the price was good – and I certainly needed a new system – but I was increasingly reluctant to go ahead. 'We'll think about it and let you know', I told him. Afterwards, when I analysed what had happened, I realised that my hesitation with the computer system was that I wasn't so much buying a product as entering a relationship. Unlike the case of the overhead projector, where I fervently hoped I'd never have to see the seller again, with the computer I was entering into a decision where I would have to work with the seller over a period of months. And I wasn't certain that I wanted to do that.

What's the moral of the story? Once again it shows that what works in smaller sales may become quite inappropriate as the size of the decision increases. In a small sale it's relatively easy to separate the seller from the product. I hated the projector seller but I liked his product enough to buy it. But, with the larger

decision, seller and product become much harder to separate. I liked the computer system but there was no way I could buy it without also buying a relationship with the seller. Because large decisions usually involve ongoing involvement with the customer, they demand a different selling style. Later chapters will be analysing what that difference is and how to use it to build lasting customer relationships.

If you're anything like the larger account salespeople that I work with, you'll sometimes feel like a very small cog in a very big and impersonal sales machine. It's often difficult to see that your work has any measurable impact. So it should be comforting to know that, as the sale grows larger, the customer puts *more* emphasis on the sales person as a factor in the decision. In a large sale, product and seller may become inseparable in the customer's mind.

The risk of mistakes

In a small sale customers can afford to take more risks because the consequences of mistakes are relatively small. In my own case I've a whole closet full of devices I've bought which didn't work or weren't half as useful as I imagined they were going to be. Right now, the top shelf contains, among other things, two automatic diallers, a fancy coffee-maker and a clock which speaks the time every hour in an improbable electronic accent. I like to think I'm not the only one who buys useless things from time to time – maybe you've a similar shelf of your own. In all my inappropriate purchases there's been a common factor – nobody else need ever know I've made a mistake. If it was a business decision, I've been able to hide it in my budget somewhere so that even Betty, our eagle-eyed and chronically suspicious budget controller, can't find out.

11

But it's different with a bigger decision. If I buy the wrong car, I can't put it on a shelf where my wife won't notice it. When I'm looking for a new computer, at least ten people in my company play some part in the decision and everybody will use it once it's installed. So if the computer doesn't work, then my whole company knows I made a bad choice. Larger decisions are more public and a bad decision is much more visible.

Customers become more cautious as the decision size increases. Purchase price is one factor which increases caution, but fear of making a public mistake may be even more important. I once had a client in London who cheerfully bought a $40 000 research project from me after just one morning's selling. The decision involved his budget and nobody else's. If the research didn't work out, he had a way to bury the cost so that he would be the only one to know. On the other hand, I had to negotiate much longer and harder with that same individual to get him to spend an additional $1500 in an area where his colleagues would be directly involved.

There's been very little research about the impact of risk on the buying decision. That's a pity, because it's an important area and I wish there were well-tested practical rules I could give you about how the increased risks of large decisions can influence your buyers. In the absence of such research, let me offer you an insight that I've found useful in my own selling. Like most salespeople, I've noticed that my prospective customers make their decisions partly on a rational and partly on an emotional basis. And I've often wondered whether, in major sales, emotional factors have a more important decision influence than rational factors. My conclusion is this. Emotional factors (by which I mean the whole range of non-rational personal likes, dislikes and pre-judices which enter into decisions) can play a key part in sales both large and small. I know the Chairman of a chain of

retail stores who still refuses to do business with a supplier because, three years ago, their sales rep inadvertently parked in the Chairman's reserved parking place. Most people have similar stories of how non-rational factors can make or break a major sale.

But does this mean you should focus on these emotional elements when you're trying to make a major sale? I'd advise you to be careful. Because of the risks involved in a large decision, a prospective customer usually discusses and shares the decision with others in the organisation. I've seen sales people who are good at influencing an individual customer emotionally, but who fail because the customer can't communicate this emotional element effectively to fellow decision-makers.

When the emotional sale backfires

I saw a perfect illustration of this a few years ago in San Francisco. The seller was a charming person with an extraordinary charismatic ability to build strong personal relationships with prospective customers. People were really attracted to him and *wanted* to do business, even if they couldn't quite explain why. For his part, he was very skilled at getting under the rational surface of customers and finding the soft emotional underbelly. So he'd say things like, 'I know that looking good to your new boss is the most important factor in this decision, and I'm here to help you do that', or 'Let's face it John, you want to do business with me because you know I *care* about you'. And I once heard him sum up a competitor by saying, 'Sure they've got a good product, but their salesman is boring as hell – and I'm fun'.

In smaller sales, where the person he was talking to could make the decision without consultation, he was successful. He had that knack of making people want to do business with him and it was very effective. However, in major sales, where his prospect had to consult with others, his record was mediocre. Fellow decision-makers weren't likely to find it convincing that they should do business just because the salesman was fun, or would make a colleague look good.

The story has a happy ending. The seller was clever enough to realise that, in a major sale, the customer has to justify the decision to others. So he changed his style. When there were multiple decision-makers he concentrated on building up the *rational* elements of his case. 'Underneath,' he explained to me, 'I'm still the same old emotional peddler. But now I realise that a prospect who's only emotionally convinced is a liability when it comes to convincing others. So, if I think that the decision is risky enough for the customer to involve other people, I now concentrate on giving good hard business reasons for buying. As a result I've become more successful in larger sales.'

In your own selling, you might find this advice useful. If the decision is visible enough to demand consultation, then it generally pays to concentrate on the rational, business elements. That's not to say that emotional elements don't exist or should be ignored. Just that the competitor who succeeds in the major sale is usually the one who has best armed the prospect with rational business justification. As the sale grows in size, rational elements become increasingly important.

Do these differences matter?

I've discussed some of the ways in which customer behaviour – and therefore selling skills – will change as the sale becomes larger. And I've given you some preliminary arguments to suggest that you need a very different selling style to be successful in the larger sale. But do these differences really matter? How can you

tell that a careful reading of the remaining chapters of this book will be a good investment?

There are several ways I could try to convince you. I could emphasise that some of the world's leading sales organisations have paid millions of dollars to have advance access to the material we're publishing here. I could quote you success stories from the many thousands of people whom we've trained in the SPIN® method. I might even show you some of the very complimentary and encouraging things which experts in selling have said about our work. But, however I do it, it's at this point in the book that I owe you some kind of tangible evidence that it's worth your while not only to read further but to read with the careful attention you reserve for something you intend to use

The Newcastle study

The evidence I'd like to present comes from some early work which we did in the Newcastle, England, branch of a major multinational. I choose this, rather than the more sophisticated studies we'll be quoting later, because we carried out the Newcastle test when the methods were very new and we ourselves had doubts about their value. It was a close examination of the results from this study which persuaded other organisations such as IBM, Honeywell, Exxon and Motorola to adopt Huthwaite's methods for training their large account salespeople.

Let's briefly review the background to our study. We had become convinced that major sales required a completely different set of skills from those being taught in conventional sales training. Our research had found, as we'll see in future chapters, that many of the standard sales techniques, such as closing, objection-handling and the use of open and closed questions were not working in the major sale. We had some preliminary research

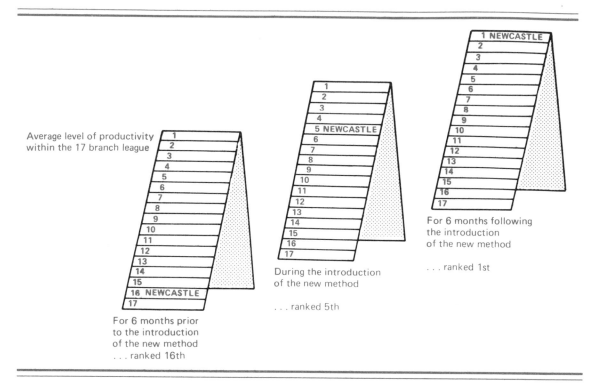

Average level of productivity
within the 17 branch league

For 6 months prior
to the introduction
of the new method
. . . ranked 16th

During the introduction
of the new method

. . . ranked 5th

For 6 months following
the introduction
of the new method

. . . ranked 1st

Figure 2.3 Productivity change within Newcastle branch

which indicated that there might be a new and more effective way to handle the larger sale but, when our story opens, we didn't have any practical evidence that our new method would be effective. Our client suggested that we take a trial sales branch and use it to test our new theories. Now, several years later, I can confess that I didn't like the idea of a practical test. I was a competent enough consultant when it came to telling people that what they were doing was wrong. But putting it right was another matter. I was horribly nervous – although at the same time I realised I'd probably never get a better opportunity to test the theories we'd been developing.

Rather than describe the Newcastle test in my own words, I'd like to offer you a more objective picture of what we found. The British journal *Marketing* published a comprehensive report on Huthwaite's work in Newcastle. Let me quote from

their account of what happened.

Confirmation that Huthwaite was heading in the right direction came when Xerox decided to put the new theories to the test. Barry Payne, who was Huthwaite's sponsor in Xerox, recalls: 'The early research was controversial. It cut across a lot of our existing ideas about selling and, understandably, raised some initial scepticism and opposition within the company. So we decided to test whether it really worked. If the theory was right, then presumably people trained according to the theory should sell better. We chose a test sales unit and trained them using Huthwaite's methods and conclusions.'

The Newcastle experiment
Xerox selected Newcastle in Britain for its test, a poor performing branch with 35 salespeople. 'We decided to measure the results of our training in two ways',

says Barry Payne. 'First we took the overall position in the branch productivity league tables, so we could compare them with other units which hadn't been trained (Figure 2.3).

'Second', explains Payne, 'we measured the number of calls needed to take each order, which was a way of assessing call quality.' The results were dramatic (Figure 2.4).

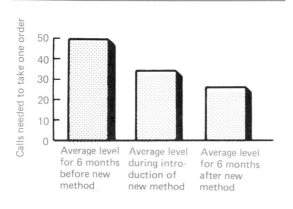

Figure 2.4 Newcastle:
changes in call/order ratio

Newcastle rose to become the top branch in the country and sustained that position until other branches were trained in the same methods. 'I remember how excited we were by the change in call/order ratio', says a Huthwaite spokesman. 'It's easy to improve sales performance in the short term by increasing *activity*, by motivating people to do more of the same thing – the so-called Hawthorne effect. The trouble with trying to increase sales productivity just by getting people to work harder, is that the effect soon wears off. We wanted to improve skills, which means getting more business from the same number of calls.'

In fact, the number of calls required to get an order was cut in half, from 48 down to 24.

But dramatic results like these have to be looked at cautiously. Barry Payne warns, 'In Xerox we commissioned an independent study which showed that while the changes in selling skill were real, out of the 16 places by which Newcastle improved, five could be accounted for by other marketing factors'.

Nevertheless, the results gave credibility to the initial research and spurred the Huthwaite team into refining and developing new models for success in capital goods selling.'

Thus speaks the journal *Marketing*. And there's not much I can add – except to say that the Newcastle study was crude indeed, in terms of the more sophisticated methods we've developed since then. But, because it was our first big success in changing the performance of a salesforce, I love it enough to forgive the study any methodological imperfections. The point for me is that the approach worked. And because Newcastle was our first real proof that we were on the right track, it's only close friends who are allowed to suggest that we got those dramatic results more through luck than through skill.

My purpose in describing the Newcastle study here is, quite frankly, to give you an incentive to read carefully. I don't expect you to believe that there was a magic method which suddenly turned a failing branch into a top performer. It wasn't like that at all – and you'd be right to mistrust any rags to riches story of that kind. Sales performance, like any other success, is largely a question of effectively focused hard work. What we did was to provide the clear focus. Success came from long, and often difficult, efforts by 35 salespeople and their managers to turn our theory into effective practice. In the chapters which follow I don't promise you an easy road to sales success. But I *do* promise a method which, with hard work on your part, can make a significant contribution to your effectiveness in the major sale.

3

Investigating: questions and sales success

Almost every sales call you can think of goes through four distinct stages as shown in Figure 3.1.

Let's take each stage in turn and examine what it is and how it contributes to sales success.

influence the rest of the sale. How important is that initial impact? How much do first impressions count? I'll be sharing with you some research which led us to conclude that in larger sales, the preliminaries have less influence on success than we'd first thought.

Preliminaries

These are the warming up events which happen before the serious selling begins. They would include such things as the way you introduce yourself and how to begin the conversation. Some people believe that preliminaries are much more important than the word suggests. I've been confidently told by a number of very successful salespeople that it's during the first two minutes of a call that the customer forms crucial impressions which will

Investigating

Almost every sale involves finding something out by asking questions. You may be uncovering needs or getting a better understanding of your customers and their organisations. As we'll see, this is much more than the simple collection of data. Investigating is the most important of all selling skills and it's particularly crucial in larger sales. Later in the book I'll describe some case studies which show that the average person in major account

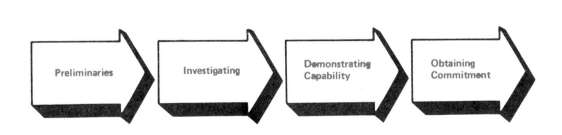

Figure 3.1   Four stages of a sales call

selling can increase overall sales volume by more than 20 per cent by developing improved investigating skills.

Demonstrating capability

In most calls you will need to demonstrate to customers that you've something worthwhile to offer. Most of us in larger sales are selling solutions to customer problems. In the demonstrating capability stage of the call, you have to show customers that you have a solution and that it makes a worthwhile contribution to helping solve their problems. Sometimes you demonstrate by a formal presentation, sometimes by actually showing your product in action and sometimes by describing some potential benefits which you could provide. But, however you do it, in almost every sales call you must convince your customer that you've something to offer. There are some very effective ways to demonstrate capability in the major sales. But, as we'll see, some of the methods for demonstrating capability in smaller sales will no longer work for you as the size of the sale increases.

Obtaining commitment

Finally, a successful sales call will end with some sort of commitment from the customer. In smaller sales the commitment is usually in the form of a purchase – in larger sales there may be a whole range of other commitments you have to obtain before you reach the order stage. Your call objective may, for example, be to get the customer's agreement to attend a product demonstration, or to test new material, or to give you access to a higher level of decision-maker. In none of these cases is the commitment an order. Larger sales contain a number of intermediate steps which we call Advances. Each step advances the customer's commitment towards the final decision. It's in this area, unfortunately, that the classic closing techniques which are taught in most sales training programmes are ineffective and may even hinder your chances of success.

We've said that the typical stages of a sales call are *preliminaries* to open the call, then *investigating* to find out facts about your customers and their needs. Next, you have to *demonstrate capability*, showing that you can help the customer and, finally, you have to *obtain commitment* to continue to the next stage of the sale. It's an offensively simple model, but we've found it very useful because it's allowed us to break calls down into a series of steps which we can study using the behaviour analysis techniques described earlier. I'll be returning to it throughout the book, using it to provide a structure for explaining some of our research findings.

The importance of each step, of course, will vary with the type of call. I remember once watching a southern banker in Kentucky selling trust services to a customer who looked like Colonel Sanders' twin brother. In that case preliminaries took up almost 80 per cent of the discussion. Before either party was ready to talk about business there was a careful 'sniffing-out' process which established some of the things essential to doing business in the rural south, such as where you were from, who you knew and whether your uncle kept horses. Only after an hour of cautious social talk was the customer ready to reveal something of his business needs.

In contrast, I recall the first time I ever went on a sales call in the garment district of New York. There were no chairs in the buyer's ofice. I assumed that meant we weren't supposed to stay long enough to sit down. On the wall behind the buyer's desk was a stark notice. 'Spit it out and get out', it read. In that call, preliminaries consisted of 'Hello, I'll be brief', from the seller and a grunt from the buyer.

Sometimes the investigating stage can take up almost the whole call. In selling consulting services, for example, you would have to find out a great deal about the customer's needs before you could determine whether there would be a basis for a business relationship. I've watched an all-day sales call by a management consultant where all but 15 minutes was spent on investigating. But, at the other extreme, I've seen calls where the investigating stage consisted of just one question, the rest of the call being taken up by an elaborate product demonstration.

So, the exact balance of the four stages will depend on the type of call, its purpose and where it comes in the sales cycle. But most calls *do* include all four stages, even if some stages are very brief.

The investigating stage

Success in the larger sale depends, more than anything else, on how the investigating stage of the call is handled. We've collected data on investigating skills from massive studies involving many thousands of sales calls. Out of all this data, we were able to derive the SPIN® process, a powerful sequence of questions which successful people use during the investigating stage of larger sales. But before we look at this SPIN® process, we should first define what we mean by a successful call.

You'll remember, from chapter one, that the method we used in our research was to:

● choose key behaviours which we thought might be important to effective selling
● watch sales calls to count how often key behaviour occurred
● divide calls into those which succeeded and those which failed
● analyse the different frequency levels

of key behaviours in successful and unsuccessful calls.

Success in the smaller sale

The effectiveness of this method rests on one deceptively simple condition – the ability to define the success of a call. You can't understand what makes an effective call unless you have some objective definition of 'success'. If this book was about simpler sales, then there wouldn't be much need to explain what 'success' means, or to worry about its detailed definition. In a simple sale, you take an order and you're successful – you don't take an order and you've failed.

So, calls in a simple sale can have one of two outcomes: an *order*, where you take the business, or a *no-sale*, where the customer turns you down. But, as the sale becomes larger, it's not so straightforward. In major sales, relatively few calls result in an order or a no-sale. Earlier I mentioned the case of a friend in the aircraft industry who went for three whole years without taking an order. At the same time, he didn't have any outright refusals which could be called no-sales. All his calls were somewhere in between. They made slow but modest progress towards his ultimate goal – an order in several years' time.

In larger sales, where only a small percentage of discussions with the customer result in an order or a no-sale, it becomes difficult to judge the success of individual calls. For example, suppose you're selling me a computer software package to help me with my inventory control. At the end of the call, I say to you, 'Look, I'm convinced that your inventory system is what we need. But I can't make such an important decision alone, so I'd like to arrange for you to come back next week and talk to our production controller'. It's clear that the call has achieved something, yet it hasn't resulted in either an *order* or a *no-sale*. It's somewhere in between. However, because it's brought about another meeting, perhaps we could say that the call has been successful.

But can we say that about *every* call which results in an agreement to a further meeting? Suppose, after you've explained the benefits of your inventory system, I say, 'I'm not sure, perhaps we could talk about it again some other time – why don't you call me in a few months to arrange another meeting'. It's quite possible that I'm agreeing to a future meeting just to get rid of you. When you call next month you won't be able to get through to me and the meeting may never happen. Just getting agreement to a further meeting isn't an adequate measure of call success.

Defining call success in larger sales

So what's the test of call success? What's the result, or outcome, which allows us to say that one call has been successful while another has failed? In our early research we took the coward's way out. We said that a call was successful if it met its objectives. I soon discovered that the amazing human capacity to rationalise away unwanted events would make this definition unworkable.

I'd been travelling with a sales rep in New York city. We made a disastrous call on a customer who became so irritated with the sales rep that we were asked to leave. Afterwards, as we stood on the pavement recovering from the experience, I was filling in call details on my research form. In response to the question, 'Did the call meet its objectives?' I had replied, 'No'. This upset the sales rep mightily. 'But I *did* meet my objectives', he protested, 'I decided, half way through the call, that we didn't want to do business with this guy because he sounded like a poor credit risk. So, rather than insult him by telling him that directly, I engineered things so he threw us out. In that way I was able to terminate the call without the embarrassment of explaining that I couldn't do business with him because his credit was poor.'

Over and over again, in our early research, we had salespeople respond in this way, telling us that whatever happened in the call had been exactly what they had planned. Call objectives can too easily be rationalised afterwards to fit events. Obviously we needed a better criterion of call success than the simple question, 'Did the call meet its objectives?'.

Our next attempt was a little better. We asked the seller to give us objectives *in advance*. We then assessed whether the call had succeeded in meeting the objectives we'd been given. In this way we were able to prevent sellers from rationalising away their failed calls. But it wasn't a perfect system. I remember one person telling me in advance that the objective of the call was 'detailed exploration of the customer's organisation structure'. At the start of the call, the customer unexpectedly revealed that, as a result of an evaluation they had carried out, they had decided to place a large order with the seller. We walked away, an hour later, with all the paperwork completed for $35 000 of business. We didn't find out a single thing about organisation structure. Yet we could hardly call it a failure just because that initial objective hadn't been met. We still needed a better way to measure call success.

The method we finally chose involved dividing the possible outcomes of the call into four areas as illustrated in Figure 3.2.

Orders

Where the customer makes a firm commitment to buy: 'We're 99.9 per cent likely to buy'

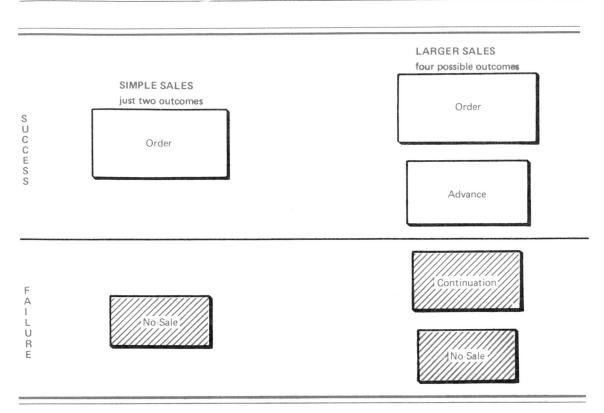

Figure 3.2   Call outcomes and sales success

would *not* be an order – as generations of sales managers have wearily pointed out to their new and inexperienced people. To be an order, the customer must show an unmistakable intention to purchase, usually by signing some kind of paperwork. Needless to say, calls which result in orders are less common in larger sales than most sellers would like. When they *do* occur, there's little doubt that they should be classed as successful.

Advances

Where an event takes place, either in the call or after it, which moves the sale forwards towards a decision: Typical advances might include:

- a customer's agreement to attend an off-site demonstration
- clearance which will get you in front of a higher level of decision-maker

- agreement to run a trial or test of your product
- access to parts of the account which were previously inaccessible to you.

All of these represent an agreement with the customer, which moves the sale forward towards the ultimate decision. Advances take many forms but invariably they involve an *action* and that action moves the sale forward. Because of that, any call which results in an advance can be considered successful.

Continuations

Where the sale will continue but no specific action has been agreed with the customer to move it forward: These calls don't result in an agreed action, yet neither do they involve a 'No' from the customer. Typical

21

examples would be calls which end with a customer saying:

- 'Thank you for coming, why don't you visit us again next time you're in the area.'
- 'Fantastic presentation, we're very impressed. Let's meet again some time.'
- 'We liked what we saw and we'll be in touch if we need to take things further.'

In none of these cases has the buyer agreed to a specific action, so there's no concrete sign that the call has caused the sale to move forward. We classed continuations as unsuccessful in our studies. This may strike you as a little unfair. After all, it seems harsh to say that a call has failed if the customer says positive things such as 'We're impressed', or 'That was a great presentation'. However, having worked closely with buyers over the years, I can no longer accept positive strokes and compliments as reliable signs of call success. Too often I've seen customers make positive noises at the end of a call as a polite way to get rid of an unwanted seller. In our studies I wanted success to be measured by *actions*, not by nice noises. That's why we classed advances as successful and continuations as unsuccessful. Success should be judged by customers' actions, not by their words.

No-sales

Our final category is *where the customer actively refuses a commitment:* At an extreme, the no-sale customer makes it clear that there's no possibility of any business. In a lesser way, it can be a no-sale, for example, if the customer won't agree to a future meeting, or denies your request to see a more senior person in the account. The test of a no-sale is that the customer *actively* denies you your principal call objective. There's not much dispute that a call which results in no-sale should be classed as unsuccessful.

Why am I making such a fuss about the different outcomes of a sales call? Surely only researchers are interested in defining call outcome – there's nothing useful here for practical salespeople. On the contrary. Our studies of top salespeople consistently showed that they had a clear understanding of these different outcomes and they used this understanding to help them turn continuations into advances. Let me illustrate this by contrasting the performance of two salespeople each selling industrial pumping equipment. First, let's look at John C. He's relatively inexperienced, having spent only a year in major sales. In this extract from an interview with him, judge for yourself whether he's clear about the difference between an advance and a continuation and whether he understands how that difference relates to sales success.

Interviewer: What were your objectives for this call?

John C.: Oh, . . . to make a good impression on the customer.

Interviewer: 'Good impression?'

John C.: Well, yes, making the customer feel positive about us.

Interviewer: And any other objective?

John C.: To collect data.

Interviewer: Data? what kind of data?

John C.: Oh, useful facts. Details about the account, just general information.

Interviewer: And were you trying to get a specific *action* from the customer?

John C.: No. As I say, it was mostly building a relationship and finding facts.

Interviewer: In your judgement, how successful was the call?

John C.: Quite sucessful I think.

Interviewer: Why do you say that?

John C.: Well, for example, the customer

said he was impressed by my presentation.

Interviewer: Did the customer agree to any actions as a result of the call?

John C.: Uh, . . . no. But I think he liked my presentation.

Interviewer: So what will happen next with this customer?

John C.: We'll meet again in a couple of months and then we'll take things further.

Interviewer: But, looking back on the call you just made, the customer didn't agree to an action which moved the sale forward?

John C.: No. But I'm sure the call contributed to building a good relationship with the account. That's why I think it was a successful call.

John C.'s reaction is typical of inexperienced sellers. He thinks the call has been successful because he received some positive strokes from the customer. But, turning to our definitions of call outcome, his call has resulted in a *continuation*. There's been no specific action agreed with the customer which moves the sale forward. Like many new salespeople, John's call objectives – collect data and build a relationship – don't directly contribute towards getting an advance. In contrast, let's hear Fred F., one of the company's top salespeople, talking about his approach to a typical call.

Interviewer: What were your call objectives?

Fred F.: I wanted to get some *movement* because I knew we'd meet competitive pressure and I didn't want to let the grass grow under my feet.

Interviewer: Movement?

Fred F.: Yes. You see, I feel that if a call's worth making it's got to *do* something – to move the sale forward in

some way. Otherwise you're wasting both your time and the customer's.

Interviewer: Could you give me an example of a call objective which shows this 'movement'?

Fred F.: Sure. In this case what I wanted was to get their chief engineer to come to our factory for a feasibility discussion with our technical people. Now that moves the sale forward – and it would also mean that while he was talking with us he wouldn't be spending time with the competition.

Interviewer: And was the call successful?

Fred F.: Yes and no. I didn't get their chief engineer because of some internal issues. So, in that sense I failed. But during the call I saw a chance to move forward in another area. The customer told me that they've just got the go ahead to build a new plant in Jersey. They're setting up a project team to write specifications and choose suppliers. So I asked him if he'd call the team's hydraulics engineer and arrange a meeting for me.

Interviewer: And he did:

Fred F.: Yes, we meet on the 23rd.

Interviewer: And that moves you forward?

Fred F.: Of course. It puts me in on the ground floor. On the 23rd I'll try to get their hydraulics man to specify us as a supplier both for pumps and specialist pipework.

Notice how Fred F.'s objectives were about getting an *action* or advance. And that he judged the call's success in terms of the movement it produced. It's that action-oriented approach which characterised the successful people we studied. They wanted advances, not continuations.

I'm often asked by sales managers for advice on how they should train their people to make them more successful in major sales. The simplest and most effective advice I can offer is this: teach your people the difference between continuations and advances and help them become dissatisfied with setting call objectives that only result in a continuation.

Even experienced people slip up here. I'm sure that many readers have come out of calls feeling good because the customer has said positive things. Yet, when you stop to think about it, the sale hasn't moved forward. Let me issue you a little challenge.

1 Think of your last ten sales calls.
2 On the basis of your own feelings about the call, decide whether you think each was successful or unsuccessful.
3 Go back over each call and ask yourself what *specific action* was agreed with the customer which moved the sale forward.
4 Look for any calls which you judged as successful but where no specific action was agreed. If you're like the top people we studied, almost all your successful calls should have an action associated with them. But if you find you've several calls which you judged as successful where no specific action was agreed, then it may be a sign that you're setting the wrong call objectives. Ask yourself whether you're accepting continuations when you should be trying for advances (see Figure 3.3).

Setting call objectives

When you're planning a major account call, question your objectives ruthlessly. Don't be content with objectives like 'to collect information' or 'to build a good relationship'. Of course these are important objectives – after all *every* call has opportunities to collect information and improve relationships. The problem is

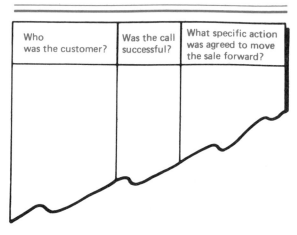

Who was the customer?	Was the call successful?	What specific action was agreed to move the sale forward?

Figure 3.3   Analysis of your last ten sales calls

that objectives of this kind just aren't enough. They lead to continuations, not to advances. In your call planning, always include objectives which result in *specific action* from the customer – objectives such as, 'To get her to come to a demonstration', 'To get a meeting with his boss', or 'To get an introduction to the planning department'. In this way, you'll be planning like the top salespeople in our study. You'll be looking for advances, not for continuations.

Back to investigating

Now let us return to our research findings. Once we had developed an objective way to classify success, we were able to watch large numbers of calls, observing which key behaviours were used more often in the calls which resulted in orders and advances. We were particularly interested in the investigating stage of the call, because our research in other areas of persuasion – such as negotiating – made us suspect that the most important of all sales behaviours were likely to occur during this stage.

It was our work in this area which led directly to the development of the SPIN® model. But the SPIN® discoveries didn't come easily. In this chapter I want to cover not only the basics of the investigating stage, but also some of the bad news – some of the models and ideas which we thought would be important to investigating, but which didn't stand up to close research scrutiny. By a conservative estimate, over a billion dollars are being spent each year training new salespeople to use the ineffective. questioning methods I'll be describing here. It's very likely you've been trained this way yourself, so you might find it useful to review some of these popular – and unsuccessful – methods for handling the investigating stage of the call (see Figure 3.4).

Let's begin by reviewing the investigating stage of the call and why it's so important. Almost every call, we've said, involves investigating – finding something out from the customer that will enable you to sell more effectively. And to investigate, you must ask questions. In the next four chapters we'll look more closely at investigating and examine:

● what effective salespeople do during the investigating stage
● which questions have the most powerful impact on customers
● which investigating skills are particularly successful in larger sales.

But first, some basics. Each one of our early studies of selling, in the late 1960s, came up with the same fundamental finding: there were a lot more questions in successful calls (those leading to orders and advances) – than in those calls which resulted in continuations and no-sales, which we classified as unsuccessful. I'd like to take credit for this simple but important discovery, but I'm told that Herodotus made a similar observation over two thousand years ago, when he noted that a common factor among most great persuaders was that they asked lots of questions.

Questions and success

There's no doubt about it, questions persuade more powerfully than any other form of verbal behaviour. That's not just in selling. Studies of negotiation, management interactions, performance interviews and group discussions – to name just a few of the areas studied by Huthwaite and other research teams – have all come up with the same basic fact. There is a clear statistical association between the use of questions and the success of the interaction. The more you ask questions, the more successful the interaction is likely to be. Having said that, I ought to add that it *is* possible for an interaction to be successful without questions. A style

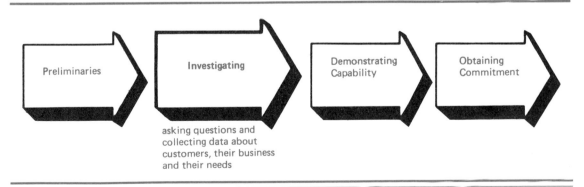

Figure 3.4   The investigating stage

high in giving and low in seeking can be legitimate and successful in certain circumstances. For instance, you can succeed without questions where:

- *You have the power*
  If I'm holding a loaded gun to your head I can probably 'persuade' you to do most things without needing to ask you questions. In a milder vein, if I'm your boss, I might use the power of my position to get what I want without having to persuade you with questions. In selling, power generally lies with the customer, but that's not always the case. I can remember when Xerox held all the patents on Xerography and – in terms of plain paper copying – had a monopoly of the market. Many of their successful sales people in those days were aggressive talkers with a high energy level. They didn't ask many questions, yet they were very successful. Their behaviour worked because, for a while, Xerox salespeople held the power – the customer had nowhere else to go. I don't see that style succeeding in Xerox today.

- *You're the expert*
  Giving can work if the customer expects and wants you to give. If, for example, you are an acknowledged expert in your field, the customer may welcome your advice and opinions. I've seen some very effective 'expert' persuaders who didn't ask many questions. The reality of larger sales is that you'll occasionally be in the expert role – when you're asked to make a presentation, for instance – and a high-giving, low-seeking style can work well.

- *You can afford risks*
  It's not that a high-giving style never succeeds. Sometimes it can be very effective. The problem about persuading by telling is that it's *risky*. You're much more likely to fail than if you use a style based on asking questions.

However, there will be selling situations where you decide to take the risk. I can remember meeting one of Honeywell's Executive Vice Presidents in a lift. I'd been trying to talk to him for months without success. 'How's it going?' he asked me. We had only six floors to travel so there was no time for questions. Instead I took a risk and said, 'Let me tell you two ways I could make it go better'. My telling caught his attention and ultimately created a sale.

Despite exceptions like these, most effective persuasion rests on the use of questions. But that raises two issues:

- *Why* are questions so important to successful persuasion?
- Are some types of questions more powerful than others?

What's so great about questions?

As a starting point, let's review some of the reasons why research shows that questions have a bigger influence on sales success than any other kind of behaviour.

1 *Questions get the buyer talking*
  The simplest possible thing to measure in a sales call is who's doing the talking. Statistically, in the successful call, the buyer is likely to be talking more than the seller. In those calls where the seller talks most, the chances of success are lower. This finding can be expressed in more technical ways. For example, we could say that the buyer talks for a greater percentage of call time in calls which result in orders or advances than in calls which result in continuations and no-sales. But the key point is the simple one that it pays to get your customer doing the talking – and the way to do it is through asking questions.

2 *Questions control attention*

Many years ago, as a student in a psychology class, I recall hearing Professor Harry Kay explain that questions were powerful behaviours because they controlled the listener's attention. I hadn't a clue what he meant, but I wrote it down anyway – just in case it might come up in a test somewhere. It didn't. But I'm glad I wrote it down because, even though I didn't realise it at the time, Harry Kay was putting forward one of the most fundamental truths about sales effectiveness. In asking questions, you control the customer's attention. Just in case this statement doesn't mean any more to you than it did to me in my psychology class, let me explain.

People's verbal behaviour can broadly be divided into two main classes – giving and seeking. Of these, we pay more attention to seeking behaviours because, early in life, we learn that seeking behaviours are the dangerous ones. Most of us can remember how you didn't have to pay attention in class while the teacher was *giving* information. But you'd be in trouble if your mind was elsewhere when the teacher started to ask questions. We learn from an early age to pay much more attention to people's seeking behaviours than their giving. Put in a more formal way, we have all learned that questioning behaviour controls the attention because, unlike giving behaviour it requires a response.

3 *Questions persuade, reasons don't*

It's said, with considerable truth, that you can never persuade people of anything. All you can do is ask the right questions which will allow people to persuade themselves. Customers, like the rest of us, are notoriously resistant to being persuaded by reasons. We found, in our negotiating research, that reasons will only work successfully in persuading people who are already on your side. That's no great discovery. If we're both in

favour of a particular political policy, you'll be very receptive to any reasons I give for supporting it. But, as we all know, if you're *against* the policy the longer my list of reasons, the more you'll find counter arguments to support your existing opinion. Successful negotiators, in our studies, used questions, not reasons, as their main persuasive tools.

4 *Questions uncover needs*

As we'll see in the next chapter, customers buy because they have needs. It's through questions that these needs are uncovered and developed. Without questions, your approach to meeting customer needs is based on guesswork – you're using 'spray and pray' selling. It's only by *asking* that you come to understand what is important to the customer and why.

I've said that the hallmark of successful sales calls is that they contain a lot of questions. So, in general, the more seeking you do, the more successful the call is likely to be. That's certainly true of simple sales. For example, we once carried out a study of selling in Hertz Corporation. Working with the Car Leasing Division, whose sales were relatively simple, we found that successful calls contained 63 per cent more questions than unsuccessful calls. In view of all the evidence on the power of questions, that's hardly a surprising finding.

Yet, during the same year, we carried out a large scale study of 1161 sales calls in a division of a corporation headquartered in Dallas. This division sold sophisticated technical equipment and their salespeople were involved in a far more complex sale than the Hertz car lease. You might expect that, in this more elaborate sale, questions would prove even more important.

Not so. Questions were only 6 per cent higher in successful calls (Figure 3.5).

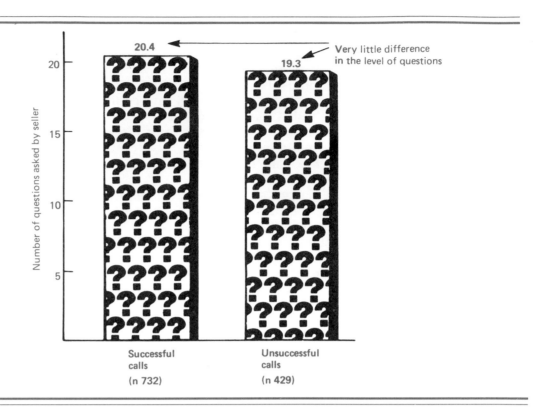

Figure 3.5   Questions and success in large sales

What does this mean? Could it be that questions don't predict success in larger sales? That doesn't seem likely. A more plausible explanation is that in larger sales some types of question are more powerful than others. So success doesn't depend on the *number* of questions asked, but on their type. It certainly seems plausible that some kinds of questions should be more powerful than others in terms of their effect on customers. That's hardly a new idea. Since the 1920s most writers on selling have suggested that it's important not just to ask questions, but to ask the right kind.

Open and closed questions

So what are the different types of question and how do they relate to sales success? The standard answer from sales writers and trainers divides questions into two kinds, open and closed:

● *Closed questions* can be answered with a single word, 'yes' or 'no'. Typical examples of closed questions would be 'Do you make the purchasing decisions?' or 'Is your existing system more than five years old?'. In some training programmes these are called *directive probes*.

● *Open questions* require a longer answer. Typical examples would be, 'Could you tell me something about your business?' or 'Why is that important to you?'. Open questions are sometimes also called *non-directive probes*.

This isn't a new concept. E.K. Strong was writing about selling with open and

28

closed questions in 1925 and there's some evidence that the distinction goes back well before then. Most writers during the last fifty years have adopted the open and closed distinction and have generally made the following points about it:

- Open questions are more powerful than closed questions because they get the customer talking and they often reveal unexpected information.
- Closed questions are less powerful although they are useful with certain customer types, such as the garrulous buyer who can't stop talking.
- Even though closed questions are less powerful, you may be forced to use them in certain types of call – for example, where very little time is available. However, some writers challenge this.
- Open questions will be particularly important to success in the larger sale, although closed questions can be successful if the sale is small.
- A general goal of sales training should be to help people ask more open questions.

These conclusions, on the face of it, seem perfectly reasonable and logical. But are they valid? As far as we could tell, nobody had ever scientifically investigated whether call success was influenced by the use of open or closed questions. It seemed an ideal area for a simple research project to assess how the mix of questions influenced the outcome of the call.

A cloudy distinction

One of the attractions of dividing questions into open and closed is that the distinction seems very straightforward. We weren't anticipating research difficulties in deciding which type of question was which. What could be easier? If a question can be answered in one word, it's closed; if it needs a longer answer, it's open. Unfortunately this distinction

proved so messy in practice that we almost abandoned the research. Let me explain the difficulty. The first example of a closed question in the definition you've just read is, 'Do you make the purchasing decisions?'. Clearly this can be answered in a single word, so it's a closed question. But how would you classify it if the customer replied, 'I make some of the decisions, but if it affects the capital budget then either the purchasing committee or central procurement become involved'? That's not a one word answer. But does that mean it's no longer a closed question? Should we judge whether a question is open or closed by the question itself, or by the length of the customer's reply? Clearly the open and closed distinction was messier than it seemed (see Figure 3.6).

We had some calls on tape and, from a preliminary analysis, we found that in approximately 60 per cent of cases where a closed question was asked, the customer gave an answer longer than one word. Thirty per cent of replies to closed questions were longer than one sentence. Turning to the other side of the coin, we found that approximately 10 per cent of open questions were answered in a single word. Obviously we were going to have a difficult time investigating the distinction. After some discussion we agreed that, for the purposes of research, we should ignore the answer and judge by the question alone. So, if the question *invited* a longer answer it was open, even if the customer gave a monosyllabic reply.

Some unexpected findings

It's easy to imagine researchers as objective seekers after truth, dispassionately investigating phenomena with an inhuman neutrality. I don't know any good researchers who are like that. We all have our preconceptions and even prejudices. I certainly had strong preconceptions about open and closed questions. Simple

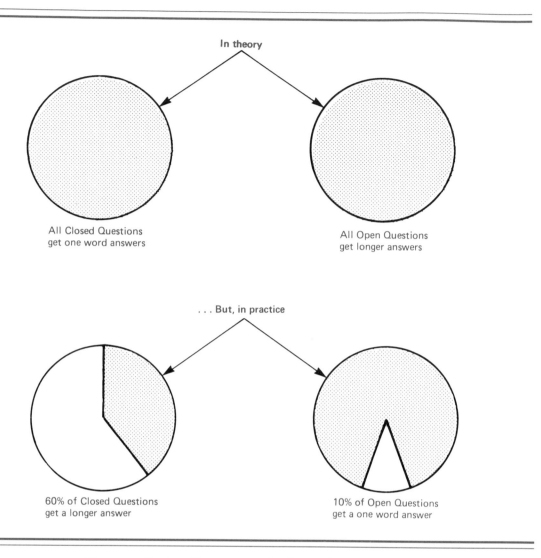

In theory

All Closed Questions
get one word answers

All Open Questions
get longer answers

. . . But, in practice

60% of Closed Questions
get a longer answer

10% of Open Questions
get a one word answer

Figure 3.6   Open and closed questions

common sense argued that open questions *must* be the powerful ones. So, once we'd overcome the methodological issue of how to define the difference between an open and closed question, I confidently expected the research would come up with some straightforward evidence to support the persuasive superiority of open questions.

Initially we watched 120 calls, counting how often sellers used questions and whether the questions were open or closed. We were astonished to find that there was no measurable relationship between the use of open questions and success. Calls high in closed questions were just as likely to lead to orders and advances. At first I didn't trust our results. Could it be that we were missing something? Was there a flaw in our research method? After coming up with such negative conclusions about closing techniques, I'd been hoping for a good commonsense positive finding about questions. I didn't expect, and didn't want, another challenge to conventional selling wisdom.

Top performers in action: a further study

Then another opportunity came up which gave us a test of our initial findings. A very successful high-tech sales organisation was carrying out a study of its top twenty salespeople. Could we, they asked, suggest any simple measures which might be used to help find differences between these high performers and average members of their salesforce. I suggested that they tracked the use of open and closed questions. It seemed a particularly appropriate measure because the company's sales training put a heavy emphasis on the importance of open questions.

Their results confirmed our earlier study. Top performers were no different in their mix of open and closed questions than were average performers. Some of the best salespeople in this very successful company didn't ask *any* open questions during the calls where they were observed. Every one of their questions could be answered with a single word. At the other extreme, several of the top people only asked open questions. Some used a mixture of the two. There was no identifiable relationship between success and the use of open or closed questions.

The company's trainers, who had carried out this study at our suggestion, were as puzzled as we were. 'I can't believe it', the project leader complained, 'we're spending hundreds of thousands every year in our basic training teaching people a distinction between questions which has nothing to do with their sales success. I don't know how I'm going to explain this to my management.' He didn't feel much better about it when I reminded him that most other companies, including his competitors, were wasting their training money in exactly the same way.

At his suggestion we set up a hasty meeting in London to review the findings and look for alternative explanations. On the way to the meeting I had an idea. We knew that both top and average sales performers used the same overall level of open and closed questions. But what if they used them in a different *order?* Perhaps top salespeople started the call with open questions to collect broad information, then moved to closed questions as the call progressed. It seemed plausible. Arriving in London with an hour to spend before the meeting I called an acquaintance who was one of IBM's top sellers. I explained my theory. 'What do you think?', I asked. 'Do *you* start with open questions and then move more closed as the call goes on?'. I was delighted by his reply. 'That's *exactly* what I do', he explained. 'Early in the call, when I'm still feeling out the customer, I like to use open questions because they give me a broad understanding of the customer and the business. But as I get deeper and I know where I'm going, I speed up the call by moving to closed questions.'

I went in to the meeting in a much more confident frame of mind. 'I think I can explain your findings' I told the project leader. He seemed equally pleased with himself. 'So can I', he said 'I've brought along someone who I think knows the answer.' Then he introduced me to one of their top salespeople. 'Kevin', he said 'tell Neil what you were saying to me about the sequence in which you use open and closed questions'. 'Certainly', replied Kevin, 'I begin the call with *closed* questions, so that I can deal with all the routine fact-finding as quickly as possible. Then, when the customer has relaxed and we've established rapport, I move to open questions so that the customer feels free to talk about whatever seems important.'

A week after the meeting, the argument was still unresolved. For every top salesperson who said you should start open and move closed, there was another who insisted that you should start closed and move open. The more I thought about it, the more the whole issue of open and closed questions seemed an unanswerable and tangled mess. Three months earlier, I'd found it very simple – open questions, which can't be answered in one word, are more powerful than closed questions. Now, after our research, I wasn't even sure I knew the difference between an open and a closed question. And I certainly didn't know which type was more powerful.

Even worse, most large companies – including all my clients – were spending a fortune teaching people a distinction which was probably doing nothing useful in terms of improving sales results. At a conservative estimate, corporations across the world were spending upwards of a billion dollars a year on an irrelevant questioning technique. Even more incredible, until our little study, nobody had ever carried out objective research to discover whether there was any validity in all that was being taught on open and closed questions.

What were we to do? Put yourself in my shoes. Here we were, a small, unknown research team finding that the rest of the army was out of step. How would we convince our clients? We faced something of a credibility issue, and it was severe enough to make us very nervous. At about this time I had an illustration of just how big our credibility problem would be. I was at a meeting just outside New York with the world's largest sales training company. The purpose of the meeting was to share research findings. During it I discovered two things:

- They didn't have much research to discuss. Although they were the largest sales training company on earth, they had done very little to measure or research any of the skills involved in selling. They certainly

hadn't looked at open and closed questions, which was the foundation of their programme. Consequently, without research to create any self-doubt, they were indecently complacent.

- They were very antagonistic about our research, mostly because it undermined their basic programme, but also – legitimately – because we didn't have very many positive findings.

Back home, licking my wounds after this meeting, I realised that the nasty reception I'd received would be typical of the way most training organisations would view our findings. It was clear that our results were not going to be greeted with open arms by the sales training fraternity. I called the research team together to decide what to do. Should we publish our findings? Or would that bring us more trouble than we could handle? Roger Sugden, one of the team members, spoke for most of us when he said, 'Let's keep our research quiet until we've found a *positive* model of questioning. Something effective enough to take the place of the old open and closed distinction'.

A new direction

We decided that the focus of our research would be to develop new and positive questioning models which could replace the old ones which were proving so unsatisfactory.

That's easy to say, but how do you do it? Where do you start after the noble intention of producing a better model of questioning skill? For weeks we all tried the classic innovative method of staring glumly at blank sheets of paper. When inspiration didn't arrive, we held innumerable inconclusive meetings to see whether that would work any better. When they failed, we did the thing which we should have done in the first place –

we went back to first principles. 'What's the *purpose* of asking questions in a sales call?' we asked. The better we understand the purpose, the better we'll understand what makes one question more effective than another. Naturally, there's a whole variety of purposes for asking questions, but the one we fastened on for the next step in our research was this:

> The purpose of asking questions in a sales call is to uncover and develop customer needs.

Put this way the statement seems obvious. However, for us it has a very important consequence. If we wanted to understand questions, we should begin by understanding needs. Writers on selling had generally assumed that customer needs in a major sale were no different from needs in smaller sales. Was this true? Was there something about needs in the major sale which was unique? And was it important enough to influence the effectiveness of different types of question? It was clear to us that our first step in developing an effective questioning model for the major sale must be to investigate customer needs.

Techniques to help your selling

Here are some practical techniques and suggestions from this chapter which can help you in major sales:

---

1   Turning continuations into advances

Success in small sales is simple – you're successful when you get an order, you fail if it's a no-sale. In larger sales, success has to be measured in terms of *advances* or *continuations*. Top salespeople set call objectives which get advances. Less success-

ful people set call objectives such as 'to collect information', which result in continuations and don't actively move the sale forward. It's a useful exercise to review your call objectives and ask yourself these questions:

- Will this call result in the customer's agreement to a clear and specific action which will move the sale forward? In other words, am I planning an advance rather than a continuation?
- If not, how can I reformulate the objectives to make something happen which will move the sale forward?
- Are there opportunities to move forward? For example, can I get access to new contacts in the account? Can I get agreement to specify or test material? Or agreement to a demonstration?
- If I can't see any opportunity for an advance, should I be making this call at all?

As a general principle, distrust call objectives such as 'to collect information', 'to keep contact', or 'to develop the relationship'. Less successful people set objectives of this kind and they result in continuations. Of course top performers *do* collect information, keep contact and develop relationships. But the primary purpose of their call is to get an advance – an action which moves the sale forward.

---

2   Asking enough questions

In selling, as in any form of persuasion, questions are the most powerful of all behaviours. Many people, particularly those concerned with sales having a high technical content, don't use enough questions when they sell. Particularly if you're in technical selling, ask yourself whether you're becoming too much of the expert – whether you're spending too much time telling customers about your products and not enough time asking them questions about their needs. There's a simple practical test you can try to find whether you are asking enough questions:

- Take a micro-cassette recorder with you into a call and tape a small sample of your behaviour.
- After the call analyse your tape. Every 20 seconds make a check mark to show who's talking – whether it's you or the customer. If you find you're talking for most of the time, then record some more calls and repeat the analysis. If you *still* find you're doing most of the talking, then you probably need to work on your questioning skills.
- Next, analyse the things you're saying on the tape. Every 20 seconds while you are talking, make a check mark to show whether you are giving information to the customer or seeking it. Again, if more than half the check marks are in the giving box, then you may be getting into the habit of being an 'expert' where you're more concerned with telling than with asking. If that's the case, your behaviour may be reducing your effectiveness and you should work on the questioning skills which are covered in future chapters.

Some types of question are more powerful than others, but forget about the traditional distinction between open and closed questions. It won't help you make larger sales.

4

Customer needs in the major sale

A few months ago I was waiting for a connecting flight in Atlanta. Browsing in an airport shop, a curious object caught my eye. It was one of those multi-bladed tools with screwdrivers, a knife and a device for extracting mysterious objects from unlikely places. It came in a neat little leather pouch and it cost about $15. Within two seconds of seeing it I was reaching for my wallet. My need developed all the way from nothing to the point of purchase in a lot less time than it takes you to read this sentence!

In contrast, the first time I bought a computer system there was upwards of a year between initial discussions about our needs and the final decision. It's in the nature of major sales that needs aren't instant. They develop slowly and sometimes painfully. Major sales require special selling skills to help this process of needs development – and those skills represent some of the most crucial differences between success in small sales and in large.

Needs in the small sale

Let's look more closely at my $15 decision and see what it illustrates about needs in the small sale. Clearly the most obvious and dramatic aspect is the faster speed of needs development in smaller sales. But there are other contrasts with larger sales that are worth noting. For example:

- It was exclusively *my* need I was satisfying. I didn't have to consult with others, as I would almost certainly do in a major sale.
- My need had a strong emotional component. I didn't have a rational use for the device and it still lies unopened on the back shelf reserved for why-on-earth-did-I-buy-that acquisitions. If I'd thought more carefully I probably wouldn't have bought it. Spur-of-the-moment decisions, often irrational ones, are more common in small sales than in large. The emotional component of needs *does* exist in larger sales but it's more subtle and more subdued.
- If I'd made a bad purchase which didn't really meet my needs, the worst thing which would happen would be the loss of $15. In contrast, a bad purchasing decision in a major sale could cost me my job.

A $15 purchase is, of course, tiny even in terms of small sales. But it illustrates some key differences between needs in small sales and in large. Broadly speaking, we can say that as the sale becomes larger:

- needs take longer to develop
- needs are likely to involve elements, influences and contributions from several people, not just the wishes of a single individual
- needs are more likely to be expressed on a rational basis and, even if the customer's underlying motivation is

emotional or irrational, the need will usually require a rational justification
● a purchasing decision which doesn't adequately meet certain needs is likely to have more serious consequences for the decision-maker.

Are these differences substantial enough to require different questioning skills when you're developing needs in a larger sale? Our research suggests that they are. We found that some of the probing techniques which were very successful in smaller sales failed entirely in larger ones.

In order to understand why questioning skills are different in larger sales, we must first be clear about the stages through which needs develop. Let's begin with a definition of what we mean by 'need'. In our research, we defined a need as:

> Any statement made by the buyer which expresses a want or concern which can be satisfied by the seller.

Incidentally, some writers have made great play of the distinction between a need and a want. A need, they say, is an objective requirement – you *need* a car because there's no other form of transport which will get you to work. A want, on the other hand, is something which has personal emotional appeal – you *want* a Rolls Royce, but that doesn't mean you need one. We found this distinction unhelpful, particularly in larger sales. When we refer to the term 'need', we use the word in a broad sense. Our definition includes both needs and wants which the buyer expresses.

How needs begin

A potential buyer who genuinely feels 100 per cent satisfied with the way things are, doesn't feel any need to change. What's the first sign – in any of us – that we have a need? Our 100 per cent satisfaction with the existing situation becomes a 99.9 per

cent satisfaction. We can no longer genuinely say that we feel absolutely content with the way things are. So the first sign of a need is a slight discontentment or dissatisfaction.

A few months ago, for example, I could honestly say I was completely satisfied with the word processor I'm using to type this book. I had no need and if you were selling word processors I'd have been a wasted call. However, while reading this, I've become more aware of a few small imperfections. The automatic spelling check is cumbersome to use. Certain editing functions are a little complicated. My dissatisfaction isn't large, but it *is* there. I'm still not a good prospect for a new word processor but the inevitable seeds of change are germinating – dissatisfaction exists and it's likely to grow.

The problem is perceived

What will happen next? Most probably it will gradually become clear to me that the editing limitations are a real nuisance. I'll perceive significant problems and difficulties, not just minor dissatisfaction. And, at that point, it will become very much easier for somebody to interest me in a new machine.

But perception of a problem, even if that problem is severe, doesn't mean I'm ready to purchase. The final step in the development of a need is for the problem to be translated into a want, a desire or an intention to act. I'm not going to buy a new word processor until I *want* to change. And when that happens, I'm ready to buy. The stages are outlined in Figure 4.1.

So we can say that needs normally:

● start with minor imperfections
● evolve into clear problems, difficulties or dissatisfactions

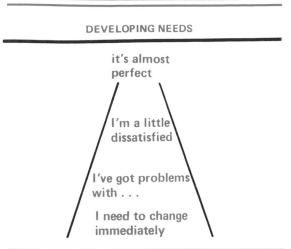

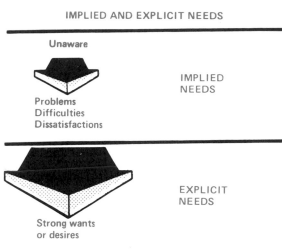

Figure 4.1   Developing needs

Figure 4.2   Implied and explicit needs

- finally become wants, desires or intentions to act.

In small sales, as we've seen, these stages can be almost instantaneous. In larger sales the process may take months or even years.

As we began to research customer needs, we looked for a simple way to express this series of stages. We decided to divide needs up into two types (Figure 4.2):

- *Implied needs* which were statements by the customer of problems, difficulties and dissatisfactions. Typical examples would be, 'our present system can't cope with the throughput', 'I'm unhappy about wastage rates', or, 'we're not satisfied with the speed of our existing process'.
- *Explicit needs* which were specific customer statements of wants or desires. Typical examples would include, 'We need a faster system', 'What we're looking for is a more reliable machine', or 'I'd like to have back-up capability'.

In this way we were able to take the continuum of needs and simplify it into just two classes – *implied* and *explicit*.

I'm always suspicious of people who introduce new jargon terms and, if I'd been reading this chapter, I'd have asked myself questions like, What's the point of dividing needs up into implied and explicit? Doesn't it just introduce an unnecessary complication? How's it going to help me sell? These are fair questions and they have an important answer. Our research suggests that in small sales the distinction between implied and explicit needs isn't crucial for success. But, in larger sales, one of the principal differences between very successful and less successful salespeople is this:

- Less successful people don't differentiate between implied and explicit needs, so they treat them in exactly the same way.
- Very successful people, often without realising they're doing so, treat implied needs in a very different way from explicit needs.

Let's look at some research evidence. In one of our studies we tracked 646 simple sales, counting how many times the customer stated an implied need during the call (Figure 4.3).

As you can see, successful calls contained more than twice as many implied needs as unsuccessful calls. This suggests that, in simple sales, the more implied needs you can uncover, the better your chance of getting the business. Confirmation of this comes from another study which we carried out with a large office products company. The company was divided into two divisions, one selling simpler low-end products and one concerned with larger sales. In the division selling low-end products, when a group of salespeople were trained to uncover more implied needs, their sales went up by 31 per cent compared with an untrained control group. So it's fair to say that, at least in smaller sales, the more implied needs you can uncover, the greater your chances of success.

But what about larger sales? Is the same thing true there? No, it's not. As the sale becomes larger, so the relationship between implied needs and success diminishes (see Figure 4.4).

What does this mean? Our interpretation

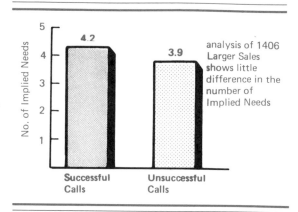

Figure 4.4   Implied needs do not predict success in larger sales

is that, in larger sales, the sheer quantity of implied needs – or customer problems – which you uncover doesn't have much influence on the outcome of the call. Instead, implied needs are just a starting point, raw material which successful people use as part of their needs-development strategy. What matters in the larger sale isn't the number of implied needs you uncover, but what you do with them *after* you've uncovered them. As an example of this, in the high-end sales division of the office products company, we carried out a test where we were able to increase the sales of 49 people by 37 per cent compared with a matched control group. Yet, unlike their low-end colleagues, these salespeople's success was unrelated to the number of implied needs which they uncovered.

Why implied needs don't predict success in larger sales

When pocket calculators were first introduced, they were offered for sale at a trade show. There was an incredible response. The manufacturer, who had brought 1500 calculators to the booth, had sold every one in less than two hours.

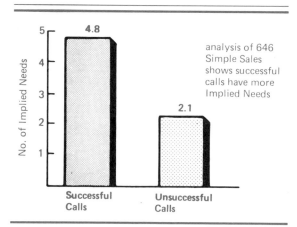

Figure 4.3   Implied needs predict success in simple sales

Hundreds of potential customers had to be turned away. Why was the new calculator so successful? Because it created instant dissatisfaction with the sheer bulk and inconvenience of large desk calculators. In other words, it generated an immediate implied need. But there was another equally important factor. The new calculator also represented a real price breakthrough, being less than one fifth the cost of the cumbersome adding machines it was designed to replace. So visitors to the trade show had a twin incentive to purchase, they had implied needs (or dissatisfaction with their existing adding machines) and an amazingly low cost for the new replacement. Combine these two points and it's easy to see why people were queuing up to buy.

But what would have happened if the new calculators had been five times the price of a mechanical adding machine instead of just one fifth? Would there still have been the same rush to buy? Almost certainly not. The reason why the calculators were so attractive was that they offered such good *value*. In other words,

they gave buyers a lot of capability for very little money.

Anyone making a decision to purchase must balance two opposing factors. One factor is the seriousness of the problems which the purchase would solve. The other is the cost of the solution. In the case of the calculators, as in many small sales, because the cost was so low it was easy for relatively superficial needs to tip the balance in favour of purchase.

The value equation

One way to think about the relationship between the size of needs and the cost of solution is the concept of the value equation. As Figure 4.5 shows, if the customer perceives the problem as larger than the cost of solving it, then there's probably a sale. On the other hand, if the problem is small and the cost high, then there's unlikely to be a purchase.

The price of a product or service is usually

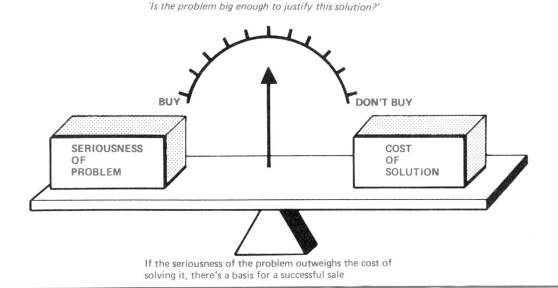

'Is the problem big enough to justify this solution?'

BUY   DON'T BUY

SERIOUSNESS OF PROBLEM

COST OF SOLUTION

If the seriousness of the problem outweighs the cost of solving it, there's a basis for a successful sale

Figure 4.5   Value equation

lower in simple sales. As a result, the size of needs required on the other side of the equation doesn't have to be so great. Implied needs may be enough to justify a purchase in the case of a small decision such as the calculator. But, if the calculator had cost *more* than conventional adding machines, then the need would have to be correspondingly bigger.

That's why you can sell in smaller sales, where the cost of the solution is generally low, just by uncovering problems, or implied needs. However, in larger sales, the need must be developed further so that it becomes larger, more serious and more acute in order to justify the additional cost of your solution. Remember that in larger sales cost isn't measured only in terms of money. As we said earlier, a bad decision can cost the buyer's job. The buyer often perceives significant risks and hassles – which can't be measured in cash terms – adding to the cost of the value equation.

Explicit needs and success

If it's true that the need has to be bigger to justify an increased cost of solution, then you'd expect that success in larger sales might be much more closely related to the number of explicit needs in the call than to the number of implied needs. This is easy to test. In the study of 1406 larger sales I quoted earlier, we also recorded the number of times the customer expressed an explicit need – which you'll remember is a specific statement of want or desire which the seller's product can satisfy. The results are shown in Figure 4.6.

Implied needs, you'll recall, were not significantly higher in successful calls. Explicit needs, on the other hand, were twice as high in the calls which succeeded. This data confirms that, as the sale grows larger, it becomes increasingly

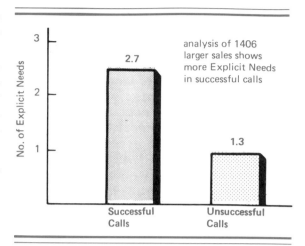

Figure 4.6 Explicit needs and success in larger sales

important to obtain explicit needs, not just implied needs.

So, in larger sales, implied needs don't predict success but explicit needs do. In smaller sales both implied needs and explicit needs are success predictors. What does this mean in terms of questioning strategy? In the smaller sale, a strategy which uncovers problems (implied needs) and then offers solutions can be very effective. In larger sales this is no longer the case. A probing strategy for the larger sale must certainly start by uncovering implied needs, but it can't stop there. Successful questioning in the larger sale depends, more than anything else, on how implied needs are developed – how they are converted by questions into explicit needs.

Buying signals in the major sale

Most people in selling are familiar with the idea of 'buying signals': statements made by the customer which indicate a readiness to buy or to move ahead. Implied needs are accurate buying signals for small sales – the more times a customer agrees to a problem or difficulty, the more likely the sale. In contrast, explicit needs are the buying signals which predict success in larger sales. We've observed that, as salespeople grow more experienced, they usually give more weight to explicit needs as buying signals in judging how successful a call has been. Less-experienced people put too much weight on implied needs. For example, here's an inexperienced seller in the telecommunications industry. Notice how he puts great emphasis on the implied needs he has uncovered as evidence that the sale has advanced.

Interviewer: . . . so you'd say the call was successful?

Seller: Yes, I think so.

Interviewer: Was there anything the customer said – buying signals, for instance – that make you feel it was a success?

Seller: Yes. They agreed they had a capacity problem during morning peaks.

Interviewer: Anything else?

Seller: They're not happy about the quality of data transmission.

Interviewer: And on the basis of those 'signals', you'd say that it's been a successful call?

Seller: I think so – after all we can help them with both these problems. I'd think there's a good chance of some business.

Here, the seller judges the call as successful because the customer raised two problems or implied needs. But, as we showed earlier there's no relationship between the number of problems you uncover in a large sale and whether the customer will ultimately buy from *you*. In this case the seller was surprised and disappointed to find, two weeks later, that the customer was talking to a competitor who, a few months after, successfully took the business. In contrast let's hear how a very successful seller from the same sales

organisation judges call success. She's one of the top five performers in her region, which contains over four hundred salespeople.

Interviewer: Was this a successful call?

Seller: Difficult to tell. I found a few problems we could solve, but until I've had a chance to go back and develop them more, I'd prefer to withhold judgement on whether we're going to get anywhere.

Interviewer: Does that mean you don't see the problems you uncovered as 'buying signals'?

Seller: Indirectly they are, I suppose. After all, you don't get anywhere unless you find some problems you can handle. So no problems means no sale – and that's a kind of negative signal – those are the worst calls. But I wouldn't really say that problems are positive buying signals.

Interviewer: In general, what *are* the buying signals that tell you a call's successful?

Seller: It's when you hear the customer talking about *action*. Things like, 'I'm going to overhaul our data network next year', or 'We're looking for a system with these three characteristics'. It's things like that.

Interviewer: You know about the difference between implied and explicit needs. It sounds like you're saying that explicit needs are a better signal than implied needs. Would that be right?

Seller: Yes. You can't just rely on problems – you've got to have something stronger. That's why I think that the big skill in selling isn't so much getting the customer to admit to problems. Almost everyone I call on has problems but that doesn't mean they'll buy. The real skill is how you enlarge these problems in order to get action. And when the customer

41

starts talking about action, that's when I hear 'buying signals'.

Here, unlike the inexperienced person, the seller puts little faith in problems or implied needs. Instead her focus is on what she calls 'actions'. The examples she offers are what, in our terminology, we would call explicit needs. Like most of the very successful people we worked with, this seller puts strong emphasis on needs development as the most important selling skill. In the last chapter I suggested that developing needs was the key function of questions. In terms of the larger sale we can now express this more precisely:

> The purpose of questions in the larger sale is to uncover *implied needs* and to develop them into *explicit needs*.

In the next two chapters I'll show how this can be done and I'll outline a successful probing strategy for the larger sale.

Techniques to help your selling

One characteristic of successful salespeople is that they can accurately predict from customer statements whether their calls have been successful. This lets them plan their time and effort effectively – they know which accounts have potential and which ones won't repay investment. One of the ways they make this all-important judgement, which we looked at in the last chapter, is by a clear understanding of the difference between advances and continuations. Another is through recognising the difference between implied needs and explicit needs. How good are you at judging the success of *your* calls? If you put too much faith in implied needs as signals of success, you may be getting a less accurate picture than if you judge by explicit needs. Test this out for yourself.

1 Take five accounts which are early in the selling cycle where you have clear evidence that a call you've made has created an *advance* – where there's been action agreed with the customer which moves the sale forward.

2 For each account:

- list the *implied needs* (customer problems, difficulties or dissatisfactions) which you uncovered
- list the *explicit needs* (customer statements of wants, desires or intentions)

(You'll almost certainly have more implied needs than explicit needs in your list.)

3 Take five different accounts. This time choose calls which resulted in *continuations* – where you haven't agreed an action which moves the sale forward. Again, for each account:

- list the *implied needs*
- list the *explicit needs*

4 Now compare the number of implied needs in the calls which resulted in advances, to the implied needs in the calls resulting in continuations.

- If the number of implied needs is almost the same, or if there are more implied needs in calls resulting in continuations, you should conclude that implied needs are not accurate predictors of call outcome. In other words, you shouldn't treat implied needs as buying signals.
- If the number of implied needs is significantly higher in the calls which resulted in advances, then it's possible that implied needs *are* buying signals in your market and that you can use the number of implied needs the customer states as a measure of how successful the call has been.

5 Now compare explicit needs in the same way.

- Are there more explicit needs in the calls which were advances? If so, explicit needs are good predictors of call success. You can safely interpret them as buying signals.

● Are explicit needs stronger predictors than implied needs?

You might, as in Figure 4.7, find that while implied needs are 25 per cent higher in advance calls, explicit needs are three times as high.

From this information, you should get some idea of whether explicit needs are more important than implied needs in your sales calls. In the next two chapters we'll look at how to use questions to uncover needs both implied and explicit.

SUCCESSFUL CALLS — Resulting in ADVANCES		
CUSTOMER	IMPLIED NEEDS	EXPLICIT NEEDS
New Tech	5	3
United Auto	4	4
Consolidated	6	4
Visigraphic	5	3
Novocom	5	4
TOTAL	25	18

UNSUCCESSFUL CALLS — Resulting in CONTINUATIONS		
CUSTOMER	IMPLIED NEEDS	EXPLICIT NEEDS
Dullsco	4	1
Boring Technologies	3	2
Slumberlands	5	1
Sleepy Systems	3	1
Amalgamated Doze	5	1
TOTAL	20	6

Figure 4.7 Implied needs and explicit needs in sales calls

5

Using questions to uncover implied needs

Clearly some questions are more powerful than others. But which ones? How could we take the all-important area of questions and divide it up in a new way which would help us build a more powerful model of questioning skill. We had defined the purpose of questions as uncovering implied needs and developing them into explicit needs. That suggests there were two types of question:

- *Uncovering questions* which asked buyers about their problems or implied needs
- *Developing questions* which took those implied needs and, somehow, developed them into explicit needs.

Some initial investigations

The idea seemed attractive enough to merit some initial research, so we approached a large multinational company. They agreed to let us travel with their salesforce, observing the use of these questions during sales calls. Our conclusions, from this preliminary investigation, were:

- Uncovering questions were more strongly linked to success in smaller sales. This wasn't surprising – implied needs predict success best in smaller

sales, so questions which uncover implied needs should have a stronger impact on success in the small sale.
- Uncovering questions were of more than one type. Further research would be required to identify these sub-types and establish which ones were most strongly linked to success.
- Developing questions were certainly important and more strongly linked to success than uncovering questions. However, it was very difficult to define a developing question and the whole category needed closer examination if we wanted to provide a workable questioning framework.

First we decided to look more closely at the simpler problem. What were the sub-types of uncovering question and how did they link to sales success?

Situation questions

Very early in the sales call, particularly with new accounts or new customers, we found that questions tended to follow an identifiable pattern. Suppose, for example, you're calling on me for the first time. What questions would you ask? You might want to know something about *me*, so you'd ask questions like, 'What's your position?' 'How long have you been here?' 'Do you make the purchasing decisions?' or 'What do you see as your objectives in this area?'. You might also want to know something about my business, so you might ask, 'What sort of business do you run?', 'Is it growing or shrinking?', 'What's your annual sales volume?', or, 'How many people do you employ?'. You would need to understand how my business was operating, so you might ask questions like, 'What equipment are you using at present?', 'How long have you had it?', 'Is it purchased or leased?', or, 'How many people use it?'.

What's the common factor in all these questions? Each one collects facts, information and background data about the customer's existing situation. So we gave them the obvious name, *situation questions* (see Figure 5.1).

Situation questions are an essential part of most sales calls, particularly those that

are early in the selling cycle. What did our research uncover about them?

- Situation questions are not positively related to success. In the calls which succeed sellers ask fewer situation questions than in calls which fail.
- Inexperienced salespeople ask more situation questions than those who have longer experience.
- Situation questions are an essential part of questioning, but they must be used carefully. Successful salespeople ask fewer situation questions. Each one they ask has a focus or purpose.
- Buyers quickly become bored or impatient if asked too many situation questions.

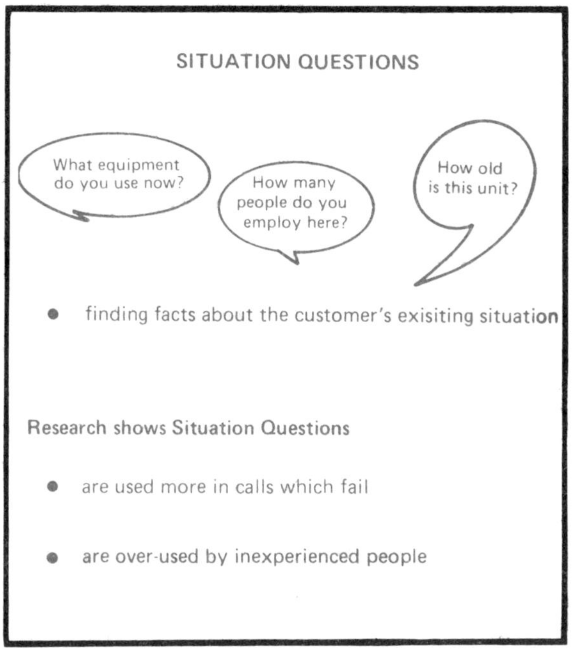

These findings are easy to explain. Ask yourself who benefits from situation questions, the buyer or the seller? Clearly it's the seller. A busy customer doesn't generally derive great delight and happiness from giving a salesperson detail after detail of their situation. And that's especially true of professional buyers and purchasing agents. I once worked for several weeks with buyers from British Petroleum's central purchasing function. Even in my neutral role as an observer, I groaned inwardly when seller after seller asked questions like, 'Tell me about your business?', or, 'What steps do you go through in making a purchasing decision here?'. I don't know how those buyers stayed sane, patiently answering the same questions day after day. I've come to believe that there's a special place in hell reserved for wicked salespeople where they sit for all eternity being forced to answer their own situation questions.

Why do we find that inexperienced salespeople ask more situation questions than those with greater selling experience? Presumably it's because situation questions are easy to ask and they feel safe. When I didn't know much about selling, my main concern in the call was to be sure I didn't offend the buyer. And because situation questions seemed so inoffen-

Figure 5.1   Situation questions

sive, I asked a lot too many of them. Unfortunately, in those days, I hadn't hit on the great sales truth that you can't bore your customers into buying. And the great fault about situation questions is that, from the buyer's point of view, they *are* likely to be boring.

Does this mean that you shouldn't ask situation questions? No – you can't sell without them. What the research shows is that successful people don't ask *unnecessary* situation questions. They do their homework before the call and, through good pre-call planning, eliminate many of the fact-finding questions which can bore the buyer.

As sellers become more experienced, their behaviour changes. They no longer spend most of their call collecting background situation information. Instead, their questions move to a different area.

Problem questions

Experienced salespeople are more likely to ask questions such as, 'Are you satisfied with your present equipment?', 'What are the disadvantages of the way you're handling this now?', 'Isn't it difficult to process peak loads with your present system?', or, 'Does this old machine give you reliability problems?'

What's the common factor in all these questions? Each one probes for problems, difficulties or dissatisfactions. Each invites the customer to state implied needs. We called them *problem questions* (as shown in Figure 5.2).

Our research found that:

- Problem questions are more strongly linked to sales success than situation questions.
- In smaller sales the link is very strong: the more problem questions the seller

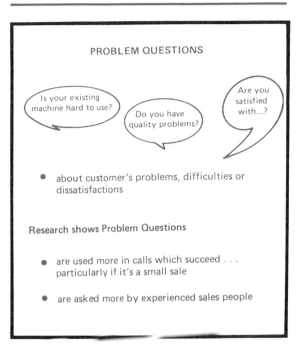

Figure 5.2 Problem questions

asks, the greater the chances that the call will be successful.

- In larger sales, however, problem questions are not strongly linked to sales success. There's no evidence that by increasing your problem questions you can increase your sales effectiveness.
- The ratio of situation to problem questions asked by salespeople is a function of their experience. Experienced people ask a higher proportion of problem questions.

Let's look more closely at what these findings mean. It's hardly surprising that problem questions have a more positive effect on customers than situation questions. If you can't solve a problem for your customer, then there's no basis for a sale. But if you uncover problems you can solve, then you're potentially providing the buyer with something useful.

47

Problem questions and experience

It's also easy to understand why experienced people ask fewer situation questions and more problem questions. I can remember how this happened in my own selling – possibly you've similar memories. When I was young and inexperienced my typical sales call consisted of as many situation questions as the buyer would let me ask. Then, when the inevitably glazed expression crossed the buyer's face, usually followed quickly by signs of impatience, I'd stop questioning and begin to talk about the features of what I had to offer. If, at that point in my career, you'd told me to ask about the buyer's problems I would have been reluctant. Even the 'safe' situation questions were making my buyers impatient – I certainly didn't want to risk upsetting them further with potentially offensive questions about problems. But the day came when I braced myself and began to ask about problems. To my surprise, instead of being offended, customers started to sit up and take notice. My calls improved. Soon I was spending more and more of the call asking about problems and less time uncovering interminable details of the situation. Most experienced people I've talked to can remember a very similar transition in their own selling.

Problem questions in the larger sale

It's true that problem questions are more strongly related to success in smaller sales, but they are nevertheless an essential part of effective probing as the sale grows larger. After all, if you can't uncover any problems to solve, you don't have a basis for a business relationship. In major sales there are, as we'll see, other more powerful types of questions. But it's problem questions which provide the raw material on which the rest of the sale will be built. When we're training major-

account salespeople, our starting point is most likely to be an analysis of how they are asking problem questions.

A harder question

Why should problem questions be so much more powerful in smaller sales than in large? Let's look at the research evidence. As you can see, in our analysis of 646 smaller sales (Figure 5.3), we found that the level of problem questions was twice as high in calls which succeeded. And, as we described in the last chapter, when we trained people selling cheaper goods to ask more problem questions, there was a significant increase in their sales.

However, problem questions are much less strongly linked to success in larger sales (see Figure 5.4).

This is because implied needs, as we saw in the last chapter, don't predict success in large sales. The purpose of problem questions is to uncover implied needs. So, if implied needs don't predict success in the larger sale, neither should problem questions.

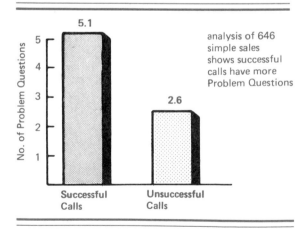

Figure 5.3 Problem questions predict success in simple sales

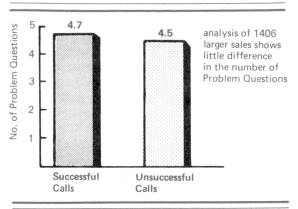

analysis of 1406 larger sales shows little difference in the number of Problem Questions

Figure 5.4 Problem questions do not predict success in larger sales

An interesting exception

Although problem questions are generally more powerful in small sales than in large, there's one interesting exception. Masaaki Imai, President of the Cambridge Corporation, carried out some experiments with us in Japan. While it's quite acceptable in the West for sellers to ask buyers about problems, this isn't so easy in the Japanese culture. There's always the risk of being insulting or offensive if you suggest that your customer – a person of status – has problems. Because of this cultural difference, Japanese salespeople ask very few problem questions compared with their Western counterparts. But, even though problem questions may be harder to ask, is there any evidence that they are linked to sales success in Japan? Working with the Engineering Products Division of Fuji Xerox, Imai found that despite the barriers to asking them, problem questions were indeed higher in successful calls. When a group of salespeople was trained in probing-skills which included problem questions, their sales rose by 74 per cent compared with an untrained control group. In this case, problem questions

were powerfully linked to success in a large sale.

Returning to our quest for an effective questioning strategy, the evidence in this chapter suggests that:

● Effective calls generally begin with *situation questions*, to uncover necessary background information. However, you shouldn't ask too many because they can make buyers bored or impatient.

● Experienced people quickly move to *problem questions*, which probe for problems, difficulties or dissatisfactions. Problem questions uncover implied needs and are more effective than situation questions, particularly in smaller sales.

So far, so good. But where do questions go from here? We've been able to divide uncovering questions up into situation and problem questions. How about *developing questions?* As you'll see in the next chapter, this proved far more difficult.

Techniques to help your selling

Customer problems, or implied needs, are at the very heart of every sale. Over the years I've helped my own selling enormously by clearly recognising this simple fact. Before I go into a call, I ask myself, 'What problems can I solve for this customer?'. The clearer I can be about the problems I can solve, the easier it is to ask effective questions during the discussion.

● Before the call, write down at least three potential problems the buyer might have and which your products or services could solve.
● Then write down some examples of *actual problem questions* which you could ask, to uncover each of the potential problems you've identified.

I'm not alone in finding it useful to list problem areas before each call. An experienced seller from a division of Kodak wrote to me, 'I've been selling for more than twenty years, and when you suggested making a list of problem areas before each visit, I though the idea was too simple to be worth the effort. But I tried and it's proved a very useful way to clarify my thinking and speed me successfully through the early stages of the sale'. Many other people have found this simple suggestion helpful. Try it. In this way you'll uncover implied needs more quickly and it will also help to prevent you from spending too much time asking unnecessary situation questions.

6

The SPIN® strategy

The prize for the most useless piece of advice on how to sell must go to the sales manager who, in training one of his poor-performing people, advised, 'If you want to be successful, all you've got to do is take more orders'. It's not that the advice is untrue – just the opposite. The problem is that it doesn't say how the poor wretch is supposed to increase those orders. Advice like this, without a how-to-do-it component, hasn't got a hope of being translated into useful action.

But how do you do it?

Judged by a how-to-do-it criterion, the second most useless piece of selling advice must be, 'In large sales you should develop customers' implied needs into explicit needs'. Again, we know the advice is true. There's ample research evidence to suggest that the chief single difference between those who are outstandingly successful in large sales and those who are merely mediocre, is that outstandingly successful people do a better job of taking implied needs and developing them into explicit needs. But the question is 'how?' In our earlier research we identified what we called 'developing questions', which we defined as any questions which extended or developed implied needs into explicit needs. But, quite frankly, that wasn't very helpful. Take a typical implied need such as, 'I've a reliability problem with

my present machine'. What developing questions is a seller supposed to ask which will turn this statement into an explicit need – a want or desire for a more reliable machine?

We realised that if we intended to produce a practical probing-strategy, we'd have to come up with something a great deal more usable than developing questions.

Preliminary conclusions

My colleagues and I had been studying the sales force of a large business machines company and we met to compare notes. Among the conclusions which we'd each come to from our various investigations were:

● In smaller sales, people could be very successful if they asked situation and problem questions to uncover implied needs and then immediately offered solutions to the problems they had uncovered.

● However, in the larger sales we'd been watching, this doesn't seem to be true (Figure 6.1). Successful sellers offered solutions very late in the call, building up the needs first. They were clearly developing implied needs into explicit needs, even though we didn't yet have a good way of describing how they were doing it.

● More than one type of question was

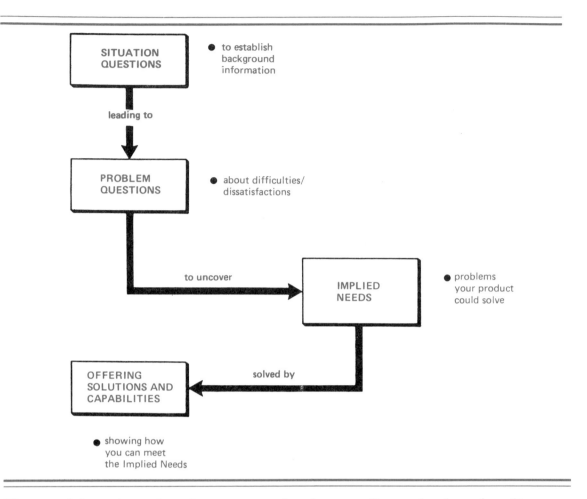

Figure 6.1   A recipe for success in the smaller sale, but for disaster in large sales

being used in successful calls to develop implied needs into explicit needs.

- Some questions seemed to concentrate on building up the seriousness of the problem. A typical example would be, 'What's this problem with reliability costing you in terms of lost production?'
- Other questions seemed to focus on the usefulness or desirability of a solution, such as, 'How would a more reliable machine help you?'
- These two types of question – the one which built up the problem and the one which focused on the solution – were at a much higher frequency in

calls which succeeded than in calls which failed.

- Generally, in successful calls, the seller would build up the seriousness of the problem first, before asking about the desirability of the solution.

From these conclusions we were able to get a rough shape of a probing strategy which sellers were using in the successful calls we observed (Figure 6.2).

What labels should we use to describe these new questions? We decided that the question which built up the seriousness of problems should be called an *implica-*

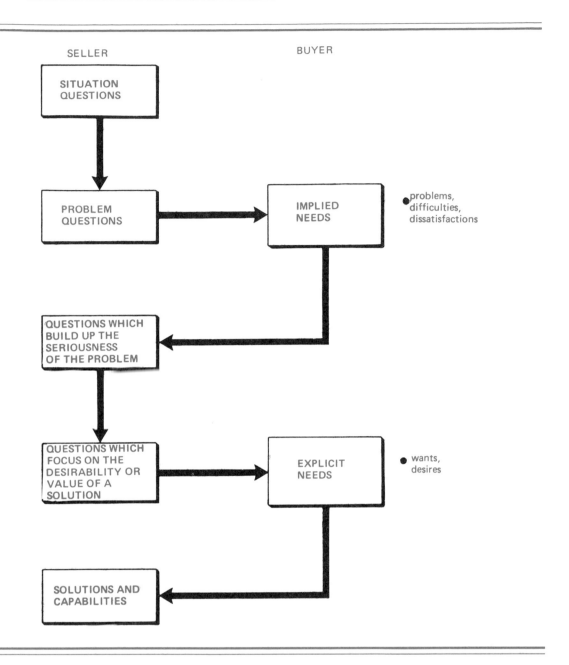

SELLER   BUYER

SITUATION
QUESTIONS

PROBLEM
QUESTIONS → IMPLIED
NEEDS ● problems,
difficulties,
dissatisfactions

QUESTIONS WHICH
BUILD UP THE
SERIOUSNESS
OF THE PROBLEM

QUESTIONS WHICH
FOCUS ON THE
DESIRABILITY OR
VALUE OF A
SOLUTION → EXPLICIT
NEEDS ● wants,
desires

SOLUTIONS AND
CAPABILITIES

Figure 6.2   A successful probing strategy for the larger sale

tion question. It wasn't so easy to name the other type. At first we wanted to use the term 'value question' for any question which focused on the desirability or value of a solution. However, this would have given us the initials SPIV for the four question types. In colloquial English a spiv is someone who stops you in the street and tries to sell you a stolen watch. On reflection, this seemed a down-market acronym for a major-sale probing strategy. We finally settled on the phrase *need-payoff* question, which gave us the far more acceptable term 'SPIN' for the four different types of question (Situation, Problem, Implication, Need-payoff).

53

Implication questions: what they are and why they are so important

We've said that successful people, once they've uncovered implied needs or problems, don't just jump in with answers. Instead they ask what, from now on, we'll call implication questions – which increase the customer's perception of the problem's seriousness. Let's see how implication questions work in practice and why they are so important to success in the larger sale.

First, let's start with an example of a strategy which *doesn't* work in larger sales. We said earlier that, in small sales, you can be very successful if you uncover problems and then demonstrate you can solve them. So a selling style based only on situation and problem questions can be very effective. However, we've also said that although many people use this style in larger sales, it isn't effective. This small example should illustrate why.

Seller: (*Situation question*) Do you use Contortomat machines in this division?

Buyer: Yes, we've got three of them.

Seller: (*Problem question*) And are they difficult for your operators to use?

Buyer: (*Implied need*) They *are* rather hard, but we've learned how to get them working.

Seller: (*Offering a solution*) We could solve that operating difficulty for you with our new Easiflo system.

Buyer: What does your system cost?
Seller: The basic system is about $120 000 and . . .

Buyer: (*Amazed*) $120 000!!! Just to make a machine easier to use! You must be kidding.

What's happened here? The buyer per-

ceives a small implied need, 'They *are* rather hard . . .', but certainly doesn't see that the problem justifies a $120 000 solution (see Figure 6.3).

In terms of the value equation, the problem isn't big enough to balance the high cost of solving it. But what if the price of the Easiflo system had been just $120 instead of $120 000. Would the buyer have reacted so negatively? Probably not – $120 is a small price to pay for ease of use, while $120 000 is outrageous. So if this had been a small sale – if the Easiflo product had cost a mere $120 – then just uncovering the implied need that existing machines were hard to use, might have been enough to get the business. As we saw in the last chapter, asking problem questions does strongly predict success in smaller sales.

In larger sales, however, it's clearly not sufficient to uncover problems and offer solutions. What *should* the seller have done? It's here that implication questions become so important to success. Let's see how a more skilled seller would have used implication questions to develop the seriousness of the problem before offering a solution.

Seller: (*Problem question*) And are they difficult for your operators to use?

Buyer: (*Implied need*) They *are* rather hard, but we've learned how to get them working.

Seller: (*Implication question*) You say they're hard to use: what effect does that have on your output?

Buyer: (*Perceiving the problem as small*) Very little, because we've specially trained three people who know how to use them.

Seller: (*Implication question*) If you've only got three people who can use them, doesn't that create work bottlenecks?

Buyer: (*Still seeing the problem as unimportant*) No, it's only when a Contorto-

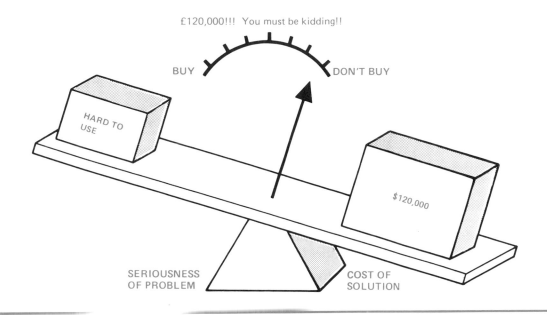

Figure 6.3 Value equation: cost of solution outweighs problem

mat operator leaves that we have trouble while we're waiting for a replacement to be trained.

Seller: *(Implication question)* It sounds like the difficulty of using these machines may be leading to a turnover problem with the operators you've trained. Is that right?

Buyer: *(Recognising a bigger problem)* Yes, people certainly don't like using the Contortomat machines and operators generally don't stay with us for long.

Seller: *(Implication question)* What does that turnover mean in terms of training cost?

Buyer: *(Seeing more)* It takes a couple of months before an operator gets proficient, so that's maybe $4000 in wages and benefits for each operator. On top of that we pay Contortomat $500 to put new operators through off-site training in their Southampton plant. So add perhaps $1000 for travel costs. You know, that's over

$5000 for each operator we train – and I gues we must have trained at least five this year already.

Seller: So that's more than $25 000 in training costs in less than six months. *(Implication question)* If you've trained five people in six months, that sounds as though you've never had three fully competent operators at any time: how much production loss has that led to?

Buyer: Not much. Whenever there's a bottleneck, we've persuaded the other operators to work overtime, or we've sent work outside.

Seller: *(Implication question)* Doesn't the overtime add even more to your costs?

Buyer: *(Realising the problem is quite serious)* Yes, we've been paying overtime at two and half times the normal job rate. Even with the additional pay, operators aren't very willing to work the extra hours – which I'm sure is one of the reasons why we're getting such high turnover.

Seller: *(Implication question)* I can see how sending the work outside must also increase your costs, but is that the only implication of sending work out? Is the quality of work affected, for example?

Buyer: That's what I'm most unhappy about. I can control the quality of everything we produce internally, but when anything goes outside I'm at the mercy of other people.

Seller: *(Implication question)* And presumably, being forced to send work outside also puts you at the mercy of other people's delivery schedules?

Buyer: Don't talk about it! I've just spent three hours on the phone chasing a late delivery.

Seller: *(Summarising)* So, from what you've said, because your Contortomat machines are so difficult to use, you've spent $25 000 in training costs this year and you're getting expensive operator turnover. You've bottlenecks in production, and these result in expensive overtime and they force you to send jobs outside. But sending jobs outside isn't satisfactory, because you're losing quality and getting late deliveries.

Buyer: When you put it that way, those Contortomat machines are creating a very serious problem indeed.

What effect has the seller had on the buyer's value equation? A small problem has now grown so much larger – and so much more costly – that a $120 000 solution no longer seems unreasonable (Figure 6.4).

This is the central purpose of implication questions in larger sales. They take a problem which the buyer perceives as small and they build it up into a problem large enough to justify action. Of course, implication questions can work in smaller sales too. A few months ago I was talking

with a friend about cars. The conversation went like this:

Friend: How's your car, Neil?

Neil: Not too bad. It's getting a bit old, but it still gets me around.

Friend: So you're not thinking of a new car then?

Neil: No. I can live a little longer with the one I've got.

Friend: *(Implication question)* But your car must be at least seven years old. Doesn't that mean you can't claim any depreciation on it for business use?

Neil: I suppose that's true.

Friend: *(Implication question)* So you're losing a couple of thousand a year in tax write-offs?

Neil: I hadn't worked it out – I didn't think it would be that much – but you could be right.

Friend: *(Implication question)* And doesn't a seven-year-old car mean that you're getting very poor mileage?

Neil: It's true that I always seem to be filling it up. Yes, it never gave me good mileage – and lately it seems to be getting worse.

Friend: *(Implication question)* And that's also leading to higher costs for you?

Neil: Yes, it's expensive to run.

Friend: *(Implication question)* And doesn't its age also mean a much higher oil consumption?

Neil: You're right. I'm putting in a litre of oil every time I fill it – it's certainly more expensive to run than I'd like.

Friend: *(Implication question)* What's the effect of age on your car's reliability?

Neil: That *is* a worry. I've only had a couple of breakdowns but – well, you know how it is – every time I start a journey I wonder whether I'm going to make it okay.

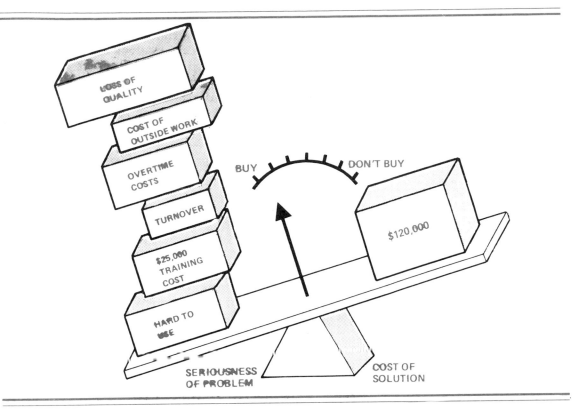

Figure 6.4   Value equation: seriousness of problem now outweighs
cost of solution

Friend: *(Implication question)* And if it *does* break down, isn't it going to be increasingly hard to find a garage which stocks spares for a seven-year-old car?

Neil: I've been lucky so far, but that's a good point.

Friend: *(Implication question)* Wouldn't it be awkward for you if you broke down somewhere and had to wait two months for spares to be delivered?

Neil: Yes, that's a worrying thought. You know, I'm beginning to wonder whether the time's come for me to change. What would you recommend in terms of a new medium-size car?

A car is certainly tiny in comparison to the larger sales which we've been talking about. But, as you can see, implication questions build up the size of the implied needs in any decision (Figure 6.5). Even in very small one-call sales, implication questions are a good predictor of success. However, as we've seen, it *is* possible to be successful in small sales without implication questions. Because of this, some people might regard implication questions as unnecessary overkill when the decision size is small.

Professionals often sell better than they realise

There's another interesting thing about this car conversation. It wasn't a sales call – my friend knows nothing about selling. He's a consulting engineer who would

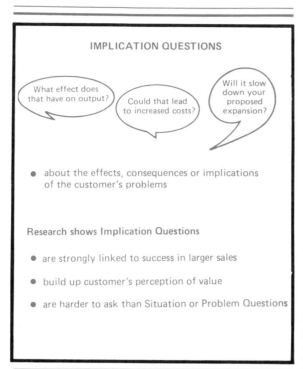

IMPLICATION QUESTIONS

What effect does that have on output?

Could that lead to increased costs?

Will it slow down your proposed expansion?

- about the effects, consequences or implications of the customer's problems

Research shows Implication Questions

- are strongly linked to success in larger sales
- build up customer's perception of value
- are harder to ask than Situation or Problem Questions

Figure 6.5   Implication questions

run away in terror if you asked him to sell. Yet here he's doing a better job of developing my needs than 99 per cent of people whose job is to sell cars. Many professional people, particularly those who have to ask a lot of diagnostic questions as part of their work, can quickly and easily learn to use implication questions to help them sell.

At Huthwaite we've designed sales training for many professional and consulting organisations and we're continually surprised at how quickly many of those we train – who think of themselves as unable to sell – can become very skilled with implication questions. We're currently working with audit partners from one of the big eight accounting firms. Nothing could be further from the image of a successful seller than the stereotype most of us have of auditors. As the old saying goes, 'Son, if you don't want the excitement and pressure of being an accoun-

tant, become an auditor'. Some of the auditors we've trained seem to share this perception of themselves and are amazed to discover that many of the questions they ask as part of their normal professional conversation will also help them be successful in a selling role.

Where implication questions work best

Implication questions are particularly powerful in certain types of sale. Obviously, as we've already seen, the main power of implication questions is in larger sales where it's necessary to increase the size of the problem in the customer's mind. But our research also found that implication questions were especially powerful in selling to decision-makers. It's often possible to achieve a positive outcome from calls on users or influencers simply by asking problem questions. With decision-makers, that's less easy. Decison-makers seem to respond most favourably to salespeople who uncover implications. Perhaps that's not surprising. A decision-maker is a person whose success depends on seeing beyond the immediate problem to the underlying effects and consequences. You could say that a decision-maker deals in implications. There have been many occasions when we've been talking to decision-makers after a call and heard them comment favourably on salespeople who asked them implication questions, saying things like, 'that person talked my language'. Implications *are* the language of decison-makers – if you can talk their language, you'll influence them better.

A more curious research finding is that implication questions are particularly powerful in high-technology sales. It's one of those odd research findings which I don't know how to explain. One potential explanation is that in older, slower-moving technologies the customer may have been buying similar products for many years and so already understands the implications. Consequently implication questions are redundant. Somehow I don't find that explanation entirely convincing. My colleague Simon Bailey, who has worked extensively in high-tech markets, raises another possibility. Many high-technology customers, he suggests, perceive decisions as very risky because of the complex and rapidly changing high-technology marketplace. Under these circumstances, they have to see the problems with their present equipment as very severe before they feel ready to risk something they perceive as new and different. I've also heard it suggested that customers mistrust high-tech sales people, so they feel more comfortable with someone who holds back and tries to understand implications than they do with someone who jumps in with premature and often inappropriate solutions. The plausibility of this explanation is strengthened by the joke: What's the difference between people who sell used cars and people who sell high-tech: *Answer:* People selling used cars *know* they are lying.

A potential negative . . .

Implication questions aren't a new discovery. People were asking them long before we began our research. Throughout history, effective persuaders have been uncovering problems and making them bigger by exploring their implications. Socrates was a master at doing this – read any of the *Platonic Dialogues* and you'll see how one of the greatest persuaders of all time uses implication questions. However, the case of Socrates also illustrates that, despite their selling power, implication questions have a weakness. By definition, they make customers more uncomfortable with problems. Sellers who ask lots of implication questions may make their buyers feel negative or depressed. Not that many salespeople end up being forced to drink hemlock,

but I do wonder whether Socrates' questioning behaviours contributed to his downfall.

That's both the strength and the potential danger of implication questions – they make problems feel worse. But is there some way to get the benefits of making a problem more acute, without the penalties of depressing your customer? That's where the next type of question comes in.

Need-payoff questions

We said earlier that our research shows successful people use two types of questions to develop implied needs into explicit needs. First they use implication questions to build up the problem so that it's perceived as more serious. Then they turn to the other type of question which builds up the value of usefulness of the solution. It's the use of this second type of question to enhance the positive elements of a solution, which prevents any unfavourable perception from customers. We called these solution-centred questions *need-payoff questions*. Basically, they ask about the value or usefulness of solving a problem (see Figure 6.6). Typical examples might include, 'Is it important to you to solve this problem?', 'Why would you find this solution so useful?', or 'Is there any other way this could help you?'.

What's the psychology of need-payoff questions? They achieve two things:

- They focus the customer's attention on the *solution* rather than the problem. This helps create a positive problem-solving atmosphere where attention is given to solutions and action, not just problems and difficulties.
- They get the customer telling *you* the benefits. So, for example, a question like, 'How do you think a faster machine would help you?' might get a

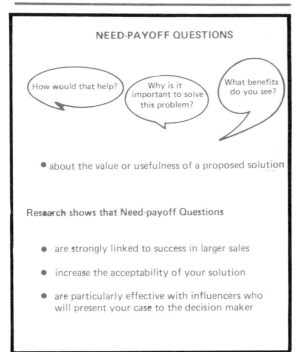

Figure 6.6 Need-payoff questions

reply such as, 'It would certainly take away the production bottleneck and it would also make better use of skilled operator time'.

Let's see how these objectives are achieved in an extract from a sales call where the seller, whose product is a telephone system, is using need-payoff questions:

Seller: *(Need-payoff question)* . . . so would you be interested in a way to control long-distance calls?

Buyer: Well . . . yes, of course . . . but that's only one of the problems I have at the moment.

Seller: *(Need-payoff question)* I'd like to consider those other problems in a minute. But first, you say you would like to control long-distance calling. Why is that important to you?

Buyer: Well . . . right now I'm receiving a lot of pressure from the controller to contain my network costs. If I could reduce long-distance charges it would certainly help.

Seller: *(Need-payoff question)* Would it help if you could restrict long-distance calling to authorised persons?

Buyer: Well, yes . . . it would certainly prevent some of the excessive long-distance usage we're getting – most of it's coming from unauthorised long-distance use.

Seller: Can we go back to issues you raised about preparing phone system management reports? *(Need-payoff question)* May I assume you'd like improvement there also?

Buyer: Yes . . . it would be a big help.

Seller: *(Need-payoff question)* Is that because it would provide you with a better method for telephone cost accounting?

Buyer: Yes, you see if we can identify departments that make calls, we can hold them accountable for their telephone charges.

Seller: *(Need-payoff question)* I see . . . is there any other way it might help?

Buyer: Umm . . . No, I think accountability is the main thing.

Seller: *(Need-payoff question)* Well that's certainly important . . . but don't you think it might also be important to know how long it takes to answer incoming calls and the total number of calls that go through each extension?

Buyer: That could be really useful.

Seller: *(Need-payoff question)* Useful for cost reasons, or is there something else?

Buyer: No, I wasn't thinking of costs. Where it would *really* aid us is in improving customer service – and in this business, that's important! Can you help us there?

Seller: Yes, we can. Let me explain how our equipment will help to . . .

In this extract, need-payoff questions have succeeded in focusing customer attention on solutions rather than problems. Even more important, the customer begins to give benefits to the seller, saying things like, 'Where it would *really* aid us is in improving customer service . . .'. It's no wonder our research found that calls with a high number of need-payoff questions were rated by customers as:

- positive
- constructive
- helpful

Need-payoff questions create a positive effect. This is one reason why we found that need-payoff questions are particularly linked to success in sales which depend on maintaining a good relationship – such as sales to existing customers.

Need-payoff questions reduce objections

In a simple sale there's usually a straightforward relationship between your product and the problem it solves. It's possible for a solution to match the problem exactly. So, for example, a person worried about fire risks for important company papers might have a problem which could be solved perfectly by the purchase of a fireproof filing cabinet.

But, as the sale grows larger, the fit between problem and solution generally becomes less straightforward. Problems in larger sales may have many parts, and the solution you offer the customer will deal with some of these parts better than with others. A problem such as low productivity, for example, may be caused

by dozens of factors. When you present your solution, you run the risk that the customer will focus on the areas you *don't* solve rather than on those you do. When that happens, as this example shows, the customer may challenge your whole solution.

Seller: . . . so, your main problem is a high reject rate on the material you use for technical tests. Our new material is so easy to use that your technicians' reject rate would be reduced by approximately 20 per cent.

Buyer: *(Raising objection)* Wait a minute. It's not only the test material which creates reject rate: there's a lot of other factors like processor temperature and developer oxidation. No. Don't give me all this stuff about easy-to-use material

What's happening here? They buyer is raising an objection because the seller's solution only deals with one facet of a complicated problem. By making claims for the product, the seller prompts the customer to raise some of the other facets and to reject the point which the seller is trying to make.

In larger sales, the problems you're trying to solve will almost always be made up of many components and causes. It's most unlikely that you, or any of your competitors, will be able to provide a perfect solution which can solve every facet of a complex problem. What's more, the account rarely expects your solution to be perfect. Sophisticated business customers look for the ability to deal with the most important elements of a problem at a reasonable cost. And, because vendors so rarely have a perfect solution, it can be dangerous for you to point out how well you can solve a problem. As in the example, by doing so you invite the customer to respond by raising the elements which you *don't* solve.

So how can you gain the customer's

acceptance that your solution is worth-while, even though it may not solve every part of the problem? This is an area where you can use need-payoff questions. If you can get the customer to tell *you* the ways in which your solution will help, then you don't invite objections. Nobody likes being told what's good for their department or business – especially by an outsider. Customers react more positively if they are treated as the experts. By using need-payoff questions you can get the customer to explain to you which elements of the problem your solution can solve. This approach reduces objections and makes your solution more acceptable, as the next example shows:

Seller: . . . so your main problem is a high reject rate on the material you use for technical tests. *(Need-payoff question)* And, from what you've said, you'd be interested in anything that can cut that reject rate down?

Buyer: Oh yes. It's a big problem and we've got to take action.

Seller: *(Need-payoff question)* Suppose you had a material which was easier for your technicians to use, would that help?

Buyer: It would be one factor. But remember that there's a lot of other factors like processor temperature and developer oxidation.

Seller: Yes, I understand that there are several factors and, as you say, an easier material is one of them. *(Need-payoff question)* Would you explain how having an easier material would help you?

Buyer: Well . . . it would certainly cut some of the rejects we're getting during the exposure stage.

Seller: *(Need-payoff question)* And that would be worth doing?

Buyer: Probably. I don't know precisely how much is lost there. It might be enough to make some difference.

Seller: *(Need-payoff question)* Is there any other way that an easier material could help?

Buyer: Those neat cassettes of yours don't need an experienced technician to set them up. Maybe that would help . . . Yes . . . if we had a material which was so easy to handle that an assistant could set it up, then the technician could spend more time on the processing stages, which could make a big impact on some of the processor problems we're getting. Hey, I like it . . .

In this example, the seller's use of need-payoff questions has allowed the *buyer* to explain the payoff and, as a result, to find the solution more acceptable.

Need-payoff questions rehearse the customer for internal selling

In smaller sales your success rests on how effectively you can convince the person you sell to. That's not always the case in larger sales. As the size of the decision grows, more people become involved. Your success may often depend not just on how *you* sell, but on how well people in the account sell to each other. In the smaller sale, you're usually there during the whole sales process. But in larger sales there are likely to be many 'sales calls' where influencers and users sell internally on your behalf and where there's no opportunity for you to be present.

A very experienced and successful sales manager in the process control industry was once asked to explain at a company conference how he had succeded in selling a multi-million dollar system to a major oil company. He said, 'The most important thing to remember about really big sales is that you only play a small part in the selling. The real selling goes on in the account when you're not there; when the people *you* sold to go back and try to convince the others. I'm certain that my success was because I spent a lot of time trying to make sure that the people I talked to knew how to sell for me. I was like the director of a play. My work was during rehearsals: I wasn't on stage during the performance. Too many people in selling want to be great actors. My advice is that if you want to make really big sales you've got to realize that even if you're a great performer, you won't be on stage for more than a fraction of the selling time. Unless you rehearse the rest of the cast, the show will be a flop'.

Most people with experience of larger account selling would agree with this analysis. It's obvious that a lot of selling goes on when you're not around, so the better you prepare your internal sponsors, the easier it will be for them to convince others in the account. The problem is how: what's the best way to rehearse customers so that they sell effectively for you? Here's an extract from a typical call on a buyer who, if convinced, will afterwards be 'selling' internally.

Seller: . . . and another way the system will help you is in reduction of inventory levels.

Buyer: Good. That's something we need to do. I'll be talking to the Finance Director tomorrow and I'll mention this to him.

Seller: Be sure you tell him that we have automatic audit tagging.

Buyer: Audit what?

Seller: It's a powerful new way to document and retrieve inventory records.

Buyer: Uh . . . okay. I'll mention it.

Seller: Tell him that we cut inventory costs in Snitch Ltd by 12 per cent.

Buyer: Because of this automatic audit thing?

Seller: Yes. And by controlling your seasonal peaks, we could do even better

here. You'll let him know that, won't you?

Buyer: Um . . . tomorrow may be a bad day for him . . . the meeting's about a city-centre property issue . . . I'll see what I can do.

Even if this buyer does talk with the Finance Director, how effective a piece of selling will it be? It will probably fail because the buyer clearly doesn't understand the product well enough to explain it.

That's not unusual. It's hard enough for salespeople to acquire all the technical and applications knowledge required to sell a sophisticated product or service. You can't expect the customer to understand in an hour something which it's taken you months to learn yourself.

But if the customer isn't going to understand your product well enough to sell it effectively, what should you do? In an ideal world, of course, you would persuade the customer to take you along to every meeting. But in real life that just isn't practical. For one thing, the customer may be reluctant to lose control of the situation by giving you direct contact with top people. For another, it would be physically impossible for you to be present in every 'sales' conversation which goes on inside an account. In a complex purchase, there may be dozens of conversations where your product is discussed between different people on the account. Even if the customer would let you, you couldn't possibly find time to attend every one of these discussions.

So there's no escaping the fact that in larger sales, an important part of the selling – perhaps most of it – will be done by your internal supporters while you're not there. That brings us back to the question of how you best prepare a customer to sell on your behalf.

This is another area where need-payoff

questions have a special use. In the next example, the seller uses need-payoff questions in a way which will help the buyer to sell internally after the call is over.

Seller: . . . and another way the system will help you is in reduction of inventory levels.

Buyer: Good. that's something we need to do. I'll be talking to the Finance Director tomorrow and I'll mention it to him.

Seller: *(Need-payoff question)* You say it's something you need to do. What benefits would you get from lower inventory levels?

Buyer: Obviously the main one is cost.

Seller: *(Need-payoff question)* Would that be the most important benefit for your finance director?

Buyer: Yes. Well . . . not necessarily. Now that I think about it, there could be another that's more urgent. At tomorrow's meeting we're reviewing our city-centre warehousing. We're using an expensive site and our Financial Director would like to close it and consolidate the inventory here. But we don't have quite enough warehousing space at this location. If your system could reduce levels at this stage by just 5 per cent, then we could close the city-centre building.

Seller: *(Need-payoff question)* And that would save you money?

Buyer: About $250 000 a year. If you've got a way to help us do that, I'll try to get 15 minutes with our Finance Director before the meeting.

Notice that in this example the seller uses need-payoff questions to get the buyer to describe benefits. In doing this, several things are achieved:

- The buyer's attention is now focused on how the solution would help, not on product details as in the earlier example. We've said that buyers can't be expected to learn about your product in enough depth to explain it convincingly to others. But buyers *can* be expected to have an understanding of their own problems and needs. Need-payoff questions concentrate on the area which buyers understand best: their own business – and how it would be helped by the solution you're posing. When buyers talk to others in the account, it's in the area of needs, not of products, that they will be most convincing and contribute most to your sales effort.
- The buyer is explaining the benefits to the seller, not *vice versa*. If you can get buyers to explain to you the value of your solution, it's good practice for when they come to give the same explanation to other people in the account. It's a much better rehearsal to get the buyer actively describing benefits to you than it would be for the buyer to listen passively while you describe the same benefits.
- Buyer's enthusiasm and confidence is increased if they feel their ideas are part of the solution. And it's that enthusiasm which will be needed to sell for you when you're not present during discussions.

In summary, need-payoff questions are important because they focus attention on solutions, not problems. And they make customers tell you the benefits. *Need-payoff questions are particularly powerful selling tools in the larger sale because they also increase the acceptability of your solution. Equally important, success in large sales depends on internal selling by customers on your behalf. Need-payoff questions are one of the best ways to rehearse the customer in presenting your solutions convincingly to others.*

The difference between implication and need-payoff questions

Both implication and need-payoff questions develop implied needs into explicit needs and, because they have a similar purpose, it's easy to confuse them. Check whether you're clear about the difference between them by deciding which is which in this brief extract from a sales call.

Implication or need-payoff question

Seller: Does the slowness of your present system create bottlenecks in other areas of the process? ☐

Buyer: Yes, mostly in the preparation stage.

Seller: And the preparation stage is an area you'd like to speed up? ☐

Buyer: Yes, we're taking too much time right now in preparation.

Seller: Because preparation is so labour-intensive, that time presumably means greatly increased costs? ☐

Buyer: Unfortunately that's true.

Seller: And what impact does that have on your competitiveness in a low margins business like this one? ☐

Buyer: It doesn't help.

Seller: So, what you'd like to see, would be a reduction in preparation costs? ☐

Buyer: That would certainly make us more competitive.

Seller: Is there any other way it would help you? ☐

The *implication questions* are examples 1, 3 and 4. Examples 2, 5 and 6 are *need-payoff questions*. Don't be too dismayed if you found it difficult to decide which was which. At first, even the Huthwaite team found it hard. In the early stages of our research, we would often come across examples of questions where we weren't sure which category fitted best. We'd write these examples up on a large white board in the office. From time to time we'd discuss these difficult categorisation problems – 'boundary issues' is the technical term – to make sure we had the closely standardised agreement between us which you need for this kind of research.

I remember, during one of these discussions, the eight-year-old son of a team member coming into the office to collect his father from work. We were in the middle of a lengthy argument about the examples on the board trying to agree which were implication and which were need-payoff questions. The child looked at the board for a moment and said, 'That one, that one and that one are implication questions and all others are need-payoff questions'. We were taken aback – we'd come to the same conclusion but we'd needed half an hour to do it. 'How can you tell?' we asked. 'Easy', he said, 'implication questions are always sad, need-payoff questions are always happy.' He's right, and since then we've called it *Quincy's rule*, after its eight-year-old discoverer. Put in a more adult way, implication questions are *problem centred* – they make the problem more serious – and that's why they are 'sad'. Need-payoff questions, in contrast, are *solution centred*. They ask about the usefulness or value of solving a problem, and that's why they seem 'happy'. This is illustrated in Figure 6.7.

Senior management of our important clients might get the wrong impression if they knew that we'd been teaching their sales forces first to ask the sad questions, then to ask the happy questions – particularly if they knew an eight year old suggested the distinction. Consequently we've never made Quincy's rule public. But, if you had trouble with the last examples, then try them again using Quincy's rule. I think you'll agree that the implication question examples, 1, 3 and 4, are sadder than the others.

Back to open and closed questions

Earlier in the book I described the Huthwaite team's finding that the traditional open and closed model of questioning isn't related to effectiveness in larger sales. I'm sure that many readers, brought up on the sensible-sounding distinction between open and closed questions, must have found our conclusions hard to believe. I can now tell you a story which may illustrate why the old open and closed distinction is less useful than it seems. I was carrying out a study of sales management coaching in a large high-technology company. As part of this study, I travelled with salespeople and watched how they put their training lessons into practice. One day I was travelling with an enthusiastic but inex-

perienced seller. During the call I recorded how often she used the different types of SPIN® questions. My results, from our first call together, were:

Situation questions	35
Problem questions	0
Implication questions	0
Need-payoff questions	0

As we know, situation questions are slightly negatively related to success. The more you ask, the less likely it is that the call will succeed. Predictably, as the call progressed, the buyer first became bored, then he became impatient and finally he asked us to leave. Afterwards, as we rode down in the lift, the seller asked me for advice. 'I was trying to ask more open questions during that call', she explained, 'Do you think I succeeded?' I was forced to reply that, unless she asked about an area which had impact on the customer – such as problems and their implications – it probably didn't make any difference whether her questions were open or closed. The sad truth is that a call which goes no further than situation questions is most unlikely to succeed. I imagine that there are tens of thousands of salespeople

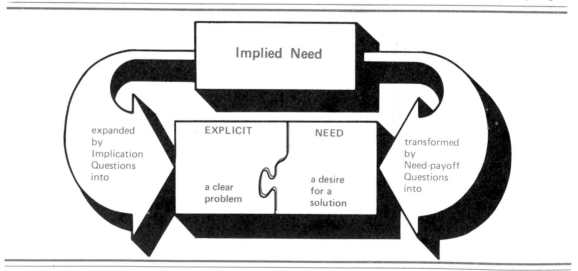

Figure 6.7   Implication question or need-payoff question?

like her, struggling valiantly to understand unproductive distinctions between open and closed questions. If only she, and all the others, understood that the power of a question lies in whether it's asking about an area psychologically important to the customer – not whether it's open or closed.

The SPIN® model

That's why the SPIN® model (Figure 6.8) is more powerful. Its questioning sequence taps directly into the psychology of the buying process. As we've seen,

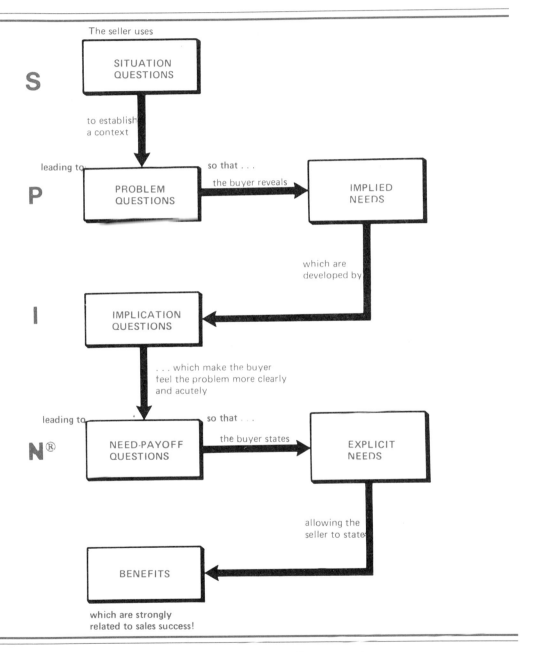

Figure 6.8 The SPIN® model

buyers' needs move through a clear progression from implied to explicit. The SPIN® questions provide a road map for the seller, guiding the call through the steps of need development until explicit needs have been reached. And the more explicit needs you can obtain from buyers, the more likely the call is to be successful.

Let's briefly review the whole SPIN® model and make a few observations about its use. Most importantly, please don't see SPIN® as a rigid formula. It's not. Selling by a fixed formula is a sure recipe for failure in larger sales. Instead, see the model as a broad description of how successful people probe. Treat it as a guideline, not a formula.

In summary, our research on questioning skills shows:

- Initially, successful people ask *situation questions* to establish background facts. But they don't ask too many because situation questions can bore or irritate the buyer.
- Next, they quickly move to *problem questions* which explore problems, difficulties and dissatisfactions. By asking problem questions they uncover the customer's implied needs.
- In smaller sales it could be appropriate to offer solutions at this point, but in successful larger sales, the seller holds back and asks *implication questions* to make the implied need larger and more urgent.
- Then, once the buyer agrees that the problem is serious enough to justify action, successful people ask *need-payoff questions* which encourage the buyer to focus on solutions and to describe the benefits which the solution would bring.

In a nutshell, that's the SPIN® model. Of course, it doesn't always work in quite this sequence. For example, if a customer begins a call by giving you an explicit need, you might go straight to need-payoff questions to get the buyer talking about how the benefits you could offer would help meet that need. Or sometimes, when you're exploring a problem or its implications, you may have to ask situation questions to give you more background facts. But, in most calls, questioning naturally follows the SPIN® sequence.

Many experienced salespeople, when introduced to the four simple questions, say, 'I could have told you that without needing a million dollars of research. It's just obvious common sense'. And, of course, they are right. We found this model by watching thousands of successful people sell. So it's not surprising that SPIN® should make immediate and obvious sense to successful people. I don't like to describe the SPIN® model as some revolutionary discovery about how to sell. It's much better to think of it as the way most successful people sell on a good day when the call is going well.

Let me invite you to think of one of your most successful calls. Didn't it broadly follow the SPIN® model? Didn't you begin by finding out something about the customer's situation? So presumably you started out with situation questions. But fairly quickly you moved into discussion of a problem the customer had. How did you do that? By asking problem questions. Then, if you think of your most successful calls, as the customer talked the problem seemed to get bigger and more urgent. Why did that happen? Presumably because you were developing the problem with implication questions. Finally, in your very best calls, were you telling the customer the benefits? Or was the customer getting excited and telling *you*, saying things like, 'Hey, *another* way you could help me would be . . .'? In most of my successful sales it's been the customer who was giving benefits. And how did that happen? Because I used need-payoff questions and I'm sure that's exactly what you've done in your successful calls too.

So you're probably using the SPIN® model already in your most effective sales. SPIN® isn't new and unexpected. Its strength comes from putting a simple and precise description to a complex process. Because of that, it helps you see what you're doing well and helps you pinpoint areas where you need more practice.

Techniques to help your selling

Most salespeople find implication questions harder to ask than either situation or problem questions. In the average sales call we studied, only one out of every twenty questions was an implication question. It seems that, powerful though they are, people have difficulty using implication questions. Yet there's good evidence (see Appendix A if you're a doubter) that if you ask more implication questions your calls will be more successful. What practical advice can we offer to help you use implication questions more often and more effectively? From our experience, the main reason why people ask so few of these important questions is that they don't plan them in advance. Here's a simple way to help you plan implication questions.

How to plan implication questions

1 Write down a potential problem the customer is likely to have.
2 Then ask yourself whether that problem might lead to other related difficulties. For instance, in the example shown in Figure 6.9, the seller is planning the call which appears on page 65. The potential problem – that the existing machine is hard to use – has four related difficulties. These are implications of the original problem.
3 Write down each of the related difficulties which could make the original problem more severe. Then note any

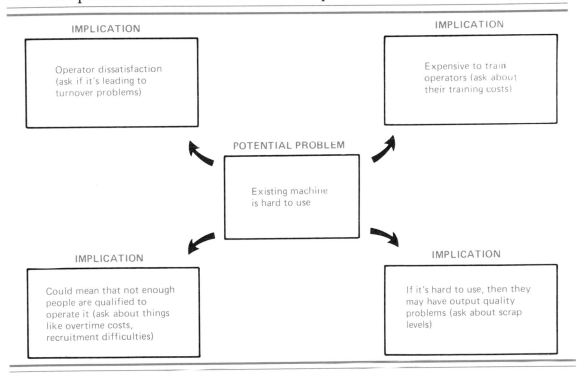

IMPLICATION

Operator dissatisfaction (ask if it's leading to turnover problems)

IMPLICATION

Expensive to train operators (ask about their training costs)

POTENTIAL PROBLEM

Existing machine is hard to use

IMPLICATION

Could mean that not enough people are qualified to operate it (ask about things like overtime costs, recruitment difficulties)

IMPLICATION

If it's hard to use, then they may have output quality problems (ask about scrap levels)

Figure 6.9   Planning implication questions

questions which these difficulties suggest to you. In this example, the seller sees that a related difficulty of a machine being hard to use is that there's a shortage of qualified operators. This, in turn suggests implication questions about overtime costs and recruitment difficulties.

It's a very simple method but it works well. Even the cleverest people we've studied find it hard to ask implication questions unless they've planned them in advance. Whether you use our simple method, or a more elaborate one of your own, the basic principle is the same. Good questions won't just spring into your mind while you're talking with a customer. Unless you plan your questions in advance, you won't think of them during the call.

Need-payoff questions

Need-payoff questions are so simple and so powerful that you'd expect them to be part of every sales call. No other type of question has so consistently positive an effect on the customer. That's why it's still a surprise to me that in almost half the calls we studied the sellers didn't use any need-payoff questions at all. It seems that, like implication questions, people find them hard to ask. Even worse, when the average seller *does* use a need-payoff question it's often at the wrong point in the call. So let's begin this section on practical techniques by looking at when *not* to ask need-payoff questions.

Avoid need-payoff questions early in the call

Some people make the mistake of using need-payoff questions too early in the call before they've identified the customer's problems. Paul Landauer of Abbott Laboratories tells the story of watching one of his salespeople open a call with the need-payoff question, 'Mr Customer, if I could show you something interesting, would you be interested?' In a less bizarre form, calls are often opened with questions like, 'If I could show you a way to increase productivity here, would you put my company on your bid list?', or 'Would you be interested in a faster way to process your accounts?' These are need-payoff questions but, asked so early in the call, they are likely to put the customer on the defensive and they'll be ineffective. The top performers we studied first built up needs before asking need-payoff questions. I'd advise you to do the same.

Avoid need-payoff questions where you don't have answers

Unfortunately, the only time when less-effective salespeople will unfailingly ask need-payoff questions is at the worst possible point in the call. For example:

Customer: *(explicit need)* I must have a machine which can give me double-sided copies.

Seller: *(Whose machine can't copy on both sides)* Why do you need double-sided copies?

Customer: *(Explaining the need)* Because it will reduce my paper cost . . . and also, if we send double-sided copies through the mail they're lighter, which cuts postage costs. There's another plus to double-sided copying too. It means we don't need so much filing space – and that's really important here.

The seller has asked a need-payoff question, 'Why do you need double-sided copies?' It would be an excellent question if the seller was able to meet the need, because it encourages the customer to explain the benefits of double-sided copying. But for this seller, who can only offer single-sided copying, it's the worst possible question to ask. As a result of the need-payoff question the customer's need grows stronger – and the seller can't meet it.

Most of us fall into this trap from time to time. We ask need-payoff questions for the needs we *can't* meet rather than for the needs we can. I'm sure you've asked the obvious question, 'why do you want to do *that*?', when one of your customers has requested a capability which you don't offer. The customer then responds to your question by telling you why the capability is important and, in so doing, strengthens the need for it.

The worst point to ask a need-payoff question is when the customer raises a need you can't meet. Conversely, the best point is when you *can* meet the need. Yet, ironically, that's when most people seem least likely to ask a need-payoff question. If the seller in the example above had a machine which offered double-sided copies do you think she would have asked that need-payoff question? Probably not. In our studies we found that when customers raised needs which the seller could meet, the most probable response from the seller was not to ask need-payoff questions but to begin talking about solutions.

Practising need-payoff questions

Implication questions require careful planning. You can't improve your skills with them unless you're prepared to invest a lot of patience and effort. In contrast, we've seen people dramatically increase their skills with need-payoff questions just by consolidating the idea with some straightforward practice exercises. Here's an example of a simple exercise which helps you practise need-payoff questions.

1 Get a friend or colleague to help you. The person you choose needn't know anything at all about selling. My son has been my 'victim' for this exercise.
2 Choose a topic where you believe the other person has a need. You might, for example, choose to talk about a new car, a vacation, a change of job or – as in my son's case – a video camera.

3 Ask need-payoff questions to get the other person talking about the benefits of the topic under discussion. In my case, for example, I asked questions like:

● Why do you think it would be good to have a video camera?
● What would it let us do that we can't do right now?
● Would anyone else in the family be pleased if we bought one?
● Do you think it would have any cost advantages compared with Super 8 film?

When you try this exercise, notice two things about it:

1 As in real life, it builds up noticeable enthusiasm in your 'customer'. A major account seller from Xerox once told me that he tried out the exercise with a girl friend, using a new car as the topic. A week later she actually *bought* a new car, explaining to him, 'your questions really convinced me I should'. The power of need-payoff questions is often visible in these very simple practice demonstrations. Watch for it.
2 Unlike implication questions, which tend to be specific to a particular customer problem, need-payoff questions have wide generality. Many of the questions you'll use in this practice exercise are the same ones you can use in real calls. There are many generic need-payoff questions like:

● Why is that important?
● How would that help?
● Would it be useful if . . . ?
● Is there any other way this could help you?

Practise the above need-payoff questions first in safe situations like this exercise. Then try them in real calls. I think you'll be surprised at their effectiveness.

7

Giving benefits in major sales

In the last two chapters, we've seen how the SPIN® model provides a strong framework for the investigating phase of the call. In this chapter I want to show you what Huthwaite's research found about the *demonstrating capability* phase. The four stages of a call are shown, again, in Figure 7.1.

Features and benefits: the classic way to demonstrate capability

Sales training and books on selling have given a lot of attention to methods of demonstrating capability. Since the 1920s

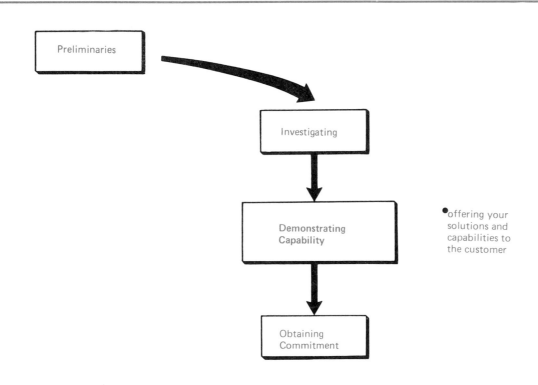

Figure 7.1   The four stages of a call

it's been recognised that some ways of presenting solutions to customers are more persuasive than others. Anybody who has been through a sales training programme in the last fifty years is likely to have been taught the terms 'features' and 'benefits' as the two ways you can describe your products or services. We're all familiar with the concept that it scarcely seems necessary to explain that *features* are facts about a product and are unpersuasive, while *benefits* – which show how features can help the customer – are a much more powerful way to describe your capabilities. If there was one area of selling where we expected our research to merely confirm the conventional wisdom it was here with features and benefits.

But we were in for some surprises. Benefits, the way you've probably been taught to use them, are ineffective in larger sales and are likely to create a negative response from the customer. And even something as simple as defining a benefit is much harder than it seems.

Features

Before looking at our conclusions, let's begin by reviewing some basics. Everybody knows what features are. They are facts, data or information about your products or services. So typical examples of features might include, 'This system has 512K buffer storage', 'There is a four-stage exposure control', or 'Our consultants have a background in educational psychology'. Features, as every writer has observed since the 1920s, are unpersuasive. Because they give neutral facts they don't help your sales presentation. On the other hand, the consensus of writers is that they don't hinder you either. What does research show? From an analysis of the number of features used in 18 000 sales calls, we found:

- Overall, the level of features was slightly higher in unsuccessful calls (which, you'll remember, were those leading to continuations and no-sales). But this difference is small enough to conclude that the conventional wisdom is right – features are neutral, they don't help the call, but they don't harm it much either.
- In small sales there's a slight *positive* relationship between the use of features and call success, so the calls higher in features were slightly more likely to result in orders and advances. This relationship isn't true in larger sales.
- In larger sales, features have a *negative* effect when used early in the call and a neutral effect when used later.
- Users respond more positively to features than decision-makers.
- In the middle of very complex selling cycles of technical products the customer sometimes develops a 'features appetite'. When this happens, the customer demands considerable product detail and may respond positively to features. It's at this stage of the selling cycle that, for example, technical experts, systems analysts and other selling support people often have a positive impact on a customer.

We also found some curious relationships between the use of features and the type of response from customers, which we'll explore in the next chapter. But, generally, our work on features confirmed what writers have been saying for fifty years. Features are low-power statements which do little to help you sell (see Figure 7.2). It's better to use benefits than features.

What is a benefit?

Our problems started when we began to investigate benefits. While everybody agrees on the definition of a feature, no two writers on selling seem to have the

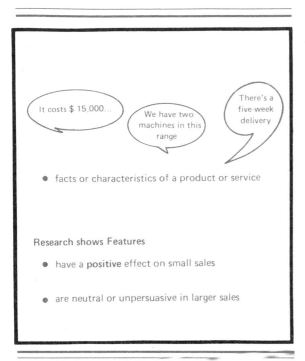

- facts or characteristics of a product or service

Research shows Features

- have a **positive** effect on small sales

- are neutral or unpersuasive in larger sales

Figure 7.2   Features

same definition of a benefit. Here are some of the many definitions Simon Bailey uncovered from a miserable month spent reading every sales book and training programme we could find:

A benefit shows how a feature can help a customer.
A benefit must have a cost saving for the buyer.
A benefit is any statement which meets a need.
A benefit has to appeal to the personal ego needs of the buyer, not to organisational or departmental needs.
A benefit must be something you can offer which your competitors can't.
A benefit gives a buying motive.

There are more. Some definitions emphasize financial elements, some concentrate on personal appeal. Others accept any elaboration of a feature, such as explaining how it can be used. My personal favourite was from a sales manager in

Honeywell who told me, 'A benefit is anything you say to a customer that's better than a feature'.

Which definition is right?

How can we tell whether any of these definitions is better than the others? There's only one valid test. The best of these rival definitions is the one which has the most positive impact on customers. Is there one of these types of benefit which occurs more than others in successful calls? We set out to test this by watching and counting how often the different types of benefit were used in calls which succeeded against those which failed. After some initial experimentation with half a dozen different definitions, we chose two for our major research test. They were:

Type A benefits
A type A benefit shows how a product or service can be used or can help the customer.

Type B benefits
A type B benefit shows how a product or service meets an explicit need which has been expressed by the customer.

We chose the type A definition because it was the most common one used in better sales training programmes. Most readers of this book will have been taught to use the type A benefit. In contrast, the type B benefit was our own definition. We chose it through watching hundreds of very effective salespeople in larger sales and analysing the types of product statements they made to their customers.

At first sight, these two definitions of a benefit seem very similar. However, their effect on customers is dramatically different, so it's worth examining each definition in detail. For example, suppose I'm selling you a computer system and I say,

'I assume you want a 32-bit system like our Suprox range because, if you ever use graphics, it will be significantly faster for you'. Have I made a type A or a type B statement? It can't be type B because I've *assumed* you want faster graphics, you haven't actually expressed a need for graphics, let alone faster ones. Take another example. You tell me that your present machine has a reliability problem. I reply, 'Because our Suprox machine uses a new generation of high-reliability components, it could solve your present reliability problem.' What kind of statement is this? This time you've certainly expressed a need. You've told me your present machine is unreliable. But have you expressed an *explicit* need? No – telling me that your present machine has a reliability problem is an implied need (a problem, difficulty or dissatisfaction). So my statement meets an implied need, not an explicit need. Once again, we should classify it as a type A benefit and not a type B benefit.

How important is the difference?

In our research we found that the type A benefit was quite strongly related to success in smaller sales but was only slightly related to success in larger sales. We'll see why later. In contrast, the type B benefit was very strongly related to success in all sizes of sale. I don't know about you, but personally I find it hard to remember which is which whenever anything is labelled A or B. I wasn't the only one who found it confusing to refer to type A and type B benefits, so we soon decided that it would be better to avoid further difficulties by putting more descriptive names in place of A and B. *We called the type A benefit an* advantage *and for the type B benefit, because it was so strongly related to success, we kept the name* benefit.

So, emerging from our research, we have three kinds of statement you can use to demonstrate capability as shown in Figure 7.3.

It's important to remember that, if you've been through sales training in the last twenty years, you've probably been taught to use a lot of type A benefits – statements here renamed as advantages (Figure 7.4). Advantages, as you can see, are more powerful in simpler sales than they are in the larger sales which are the subject of this book. Almost certainly, you'll find some confusion between the definition of benefit we're using here and the definitions you've learned in the past.

Most salespeople I've worked with hate quibbling about definitions. I don't blame them. But, in this case, definitions are vitally important. Later in the book, you'll see evaluation studies where, by getting salespeople to use benefits rather than advantages, we've been able to produce increases in sales volume in excess of 30 per cent. That's more than a quibble! When the definition is derived from choosing the statements which have highest impact on customers, then we're not just playing with words. Because these differences are so important, I'd like to give you the chance to test your understanding of them by working through this short transcript. See if you can pick out which of the ten product statements are *features, advantages* or *benefits.* Then check your results with the answers at the end of the chapter.

Is it a feature, advantage, or benefit?

Seller: And another thing about the system is that it has balanced voltage stabilisation. ☐

Buyer: Oh, what does that do?

Seller: It protects you from current surges, so that you won't lose valuable data if ☐

BEHAVIOUR	DEFINITION	IMPACT	
		On Small Sales	On Larger Sales
FEATURES	describe facts, data, product characteristics	slightly positive	neutral or slightly negative
ADVANTAGES (Type A Benefits)	show how products, services or their Features can be used or can help the customer	positive	slightly positive
BENEFITS (Type B Benefits)	show how products or services meet Explicit Needs expressed by the customer	very positive	very positive

Figure 7.3   Features, advantages and benefits

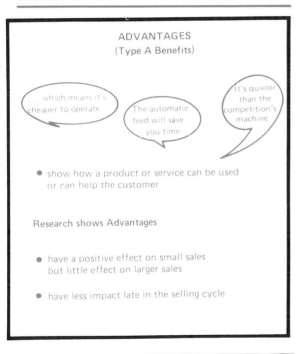

Figure 7.4   Advantages

you have a voltage fluctuation.

Buyer: That isn't necessary here. This building is wired for scientific use, so there's inbuilt voltage protection.

Seller: But I'm sure you'll find the backup memory useful. It means that even in the event of an operator error wiping you main files, you'll always have automatic back up – so you'll never run the risk of losing key data.

Buyer: And how much does this configuration cost?

Seller: The basic core system costs $78 000.

Buyer: And is it compatible with our optical readers? I need to be able to read source data straight into memory.

Seller: Yes, you'll be able to

read your present data without any conversion, so if you want to read direct into memory you'll be able to do that.

Buyer: That's good. How about error rates? I must have a less than one in 100 000.

Seller: Then you'll be glad to hear that the system has one of the lowest error rates on the market – less than 1 in 1 500 000 – which easily meets your demand.

Buyer: Fine.

Seller: And because of the low error rate, you can also use the system to re-run and verify data from your other processing sources – thus saving you the cost of a separate verification process.

Buyer: I'm not sure about that. We have other security issues around data verification which means we wouldn't be permitted to take data from our other sources.

Seller: On the subject of security, this system has eight levels of possible coding built in.

Buyer: Are they user-determined?

Seller: On five levels – the other three are randomised or time-based.

Buyer: Time-based?

Seller: Oh yes. You see, the big plus of a time-based system for an organisation like yours is that you can simultaneously and automatically roll over access codes between operating units – which means that your operators don't have to

memorise new codes, yet it's almost impossible for outsiders to break in.

Now that you're familiar with the rather special way we use the terms 'advantages' and 'benefits', let's examine the research evidence in more detail.

Why advantages work in small sales

We've said that advantages – statements which show how your product can be used or can help the customer – have a much more positive impact on small sales than on larger ones. Why? It seems odd that the impact should be so much less in the large sale. The most probable answer goes back to the model we were discussing in chapter six. Remember that we showed how you could be very successful in smaller sales by using situation and problem questions to uncover implied needs and then offering solutions (Figure 7.5).

What would those solutions be in terms of features, advantages and benefits? They can't be benefits because, as we've seen, you can only give a benefit if you address an explicit need, which the customer has expressed. In this case the solutions are offered to implied needs, so they must be either features or advantages. We've seen that offering solutions to implied needs isn't effective in larger sales. So this use of features and advantages, which can work perfectly well in the small sale, is likely to be ineffective as the sale grows larger.

The power of benefits

That's why our research found that benefits were so much more powerful in larger sales (see Figure 7.6). To give a benefit, you must have an explicit need.

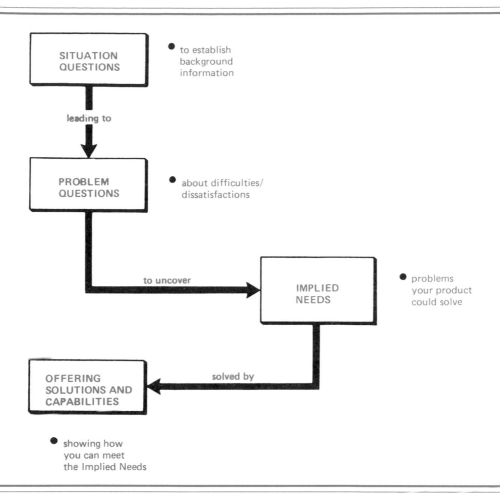

Figure 7.5   A recipe for success in the smaller sale, but for disaster in large sales

But, in order to get the explicit need, you normally must first develop it from an implied need using implication and need-payoff questions. Using benefits, as we define them, can't be divorced from the way you develop needs. My colleagues at Huthwaite are often asked when we run training programmes for advice on how to use more benefits. Our reply is simple, 'Do a good job of developing explicit needs and the benefits almost look after themselves'. If you can get your customers to say 'I want it', it's not difficult to give a benefit by replying, 'We can give it to you'.

Benefits and call success

One of our early studies which confirmed the power of benefits was carried out in a number of high-technology companies across Europe and North America. We compared the level of benefits in 5000 calls with the outcome of each call. The results are shown in Figure 7.7.

We found that benefits (and remember that our definition of a benefit is a statement which shows how you can

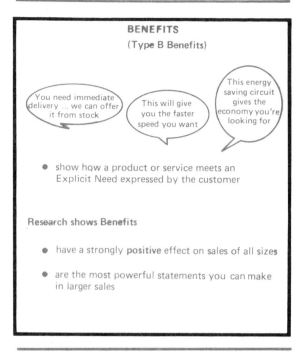

BENEFITS
(Type B Benefits)

- show how a product or service meets an Explicit Need expressed by the customer

Research shows Benefits

- have a strongly positive effect on sales of all sizes
- are the most powerful statements you can make in larger sales

Figure 7.6   Benefits

meet an *expressed explicit need)* were significantly higher in calls leading to orders and advances. In contrast, the level of advantages (showing how your product can help or be used – what many of us have been taught to call 'benefits') was not significantly different in successful and unsuccessful calls.

Features, advantages and benefits in the longer selling cycle

One of the curious findings from our research was that the impact of features, advantages and benefits on the customer is not constant throughout the selling cycle (Figure 7.8).

We were working with one of the world's leading business-machines companies and part of our investigation involved

measuring the effect of sales behaviours at different points of the cycle. The average selling cycle, in this organisation was 7.8 calls long. Company researchers, working with Huthwaite, accompanied salespeople into calls at different points in the selling cycle. They observed the frequency with which each seller used features, advantages and benefits, then compared this data with the outcome of each call. To be technical for a moment, the vertical axis of the graph actually shows the significance level of each behaviour measured by a battery of non-parametric tests. In simpler terms, the higher a behaviour comes on that axis, the more it's likely to help you sell.

As you can see, features have a low impact on the customer throughout the selling cycle. Benefits, at the other extreme, have a high impact whenever they are used. The unusual behaviour is advantages. We found that early in the cycle, particularly during the first call, advantages had a moderately good statistical relationship to call success. That's another way to say that advantages had a positive impact on the customer during the first call – sellers who used a lot of advantages were likely to get an advance rather than a continuation or no-sale. However, as the cycle progressed, advantages had a decreasing effect on the customer until, as the end of the cycle approached, they were no more powerful than features.

Why do advantages run out of steam?

To be honest, I'm not sure why advantages are more effective early in the cycle than late. It's one of those findings which the Huthwaite research team still argues about whenever we get together. Possibly it's because, at a first meeting, the customer expects to hear about the product rather than to discuss needs. I'm sure you've made first visits to customers

Calls were divided into:

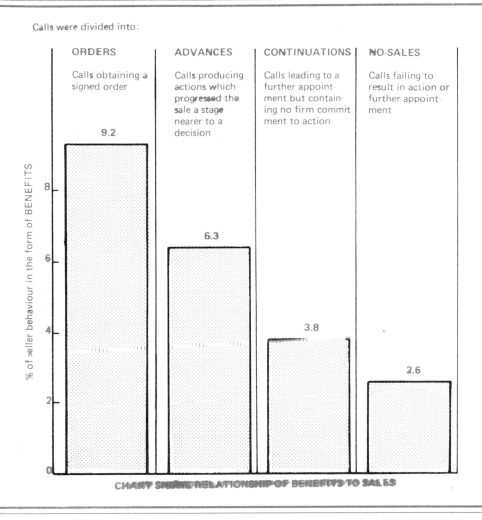

Figure 7.7   Relationship of benefits to outcomes in 5000
high-technology calls

who start off the call by saying 'Now, tell me all about this product of yours . . .' I've certainly had customers who don't want to discuss needs until they know more about what I've got to offer.

Another possibility is that many of the sellers who jump in early with advantages do so because they are genuinely enthusiastic about their products. They can't wait to start talking solutions. In the short term, their enthusiasm carries them along, at least to the point where the customer agrees to proceed to a further step in the selling cycle. However, if they continue a product-centred approach as the cycle progresses, they aren't responsive to customer needs and therefore become less effective.

Yet another possibility is that advantages, as we've seen earlier, are very quickly forgotten after the call. Consequently their effect is temporary while, in contrast, benefits continue to have an impact between calls because their link to explicit

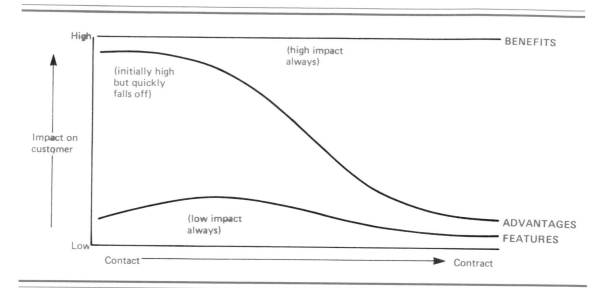

Figure 7.8   Features, advantages and benefits across the selling cycle

needs helps customers to remember them.

Whatever the reason, I'm sure you've seen cases in your own company of this phenomenon in action. A typical example is the pushy, aggressive individual who's much more interested in selling product than in meeting customer needs. This kind of person will frequently be very successful in the early stages of the sale. I'm sure you've listened, as I have, to the stories these people tell about how they've just had a first meeting with a new customer and impressed them tremendously by the way they put the product across and showed how it could solve all the customer's problems. But how many of these promising beginnings turn into orders? Fewer than you'd expect. And a very likely reason is that the seller's high advantage style has helped early in the cycle but run out of steam as the sale progressed. But, whatever the explanations, the research is giving us a simple but important message. Advantages are less powerful than benefits all through the selling cycle. It never pays to offer an advantage if you can go that bit further and offer a benefit.

Selling new products

There's one area of demonstrating capability which is generally badly handled, even by experienced salespeople. It happens to be an area vital to most organisations' success and it's a source of perennial frustration and disappointment to senior management. The area I'm talking about is the new product launch. Over and over again, my Huthwaite colleagues and I are asked by top management to help explain why a new product has failed to meet its initial sales target. 'What's wrong?', they ask, 'We were sure our projections were realistic and now, six months into the launch, we're less than 50 per cent of plan. Is it the product? Is it the salesforce? What's going wrong?' From the many product launches we've studied, one constant fact emerges. The biggest single cause of poor results early in a product's life can be explained in terms of features, advantages and benefits.

When a product is new, how does product marketing generally communicate it to the sales force? They call people together and tell them about what an exciting new product is coming. They explain all the features and advantages – all the bells and whistles. And what does the sales force then do? They become excited about the product and go out to sell it. And, when they are in front of the customers, how do they behave? They communicate the product in exactly the same way it was communicated to them. Instead of asking questions to develop needs, they jump in with all the exciting features and advantages which the new product possesses.

As you can see from this composite data (Figure 7.9), taken from a number of product launches combined, the average number of features and advantages given when selling new products is more than three times the level given by the same salespeople when selling existing products. The evidence suggests that the sellers' attention is much more on the product than on their customers. To be frank, I've done it myself – you've probably done the same thing too. Whenever Huthwaite launches a new product we all get excited and enthusiastic, we can't wait to tell our clients all about it. And, like so many other companies, we wonder why – despite our enthusiasm – we're not making sales. We now understand that it's precisely *because* of our enthusiasm that we have a problem. Our enthusiasm has led us to become product centred and to describe features and advantages. As we've seen in this chapter, that's not an effective strategy for the major sale.

We had an interesting opportunity to test whether something as simple as excessive features and advantages could really account for the slow growth of new

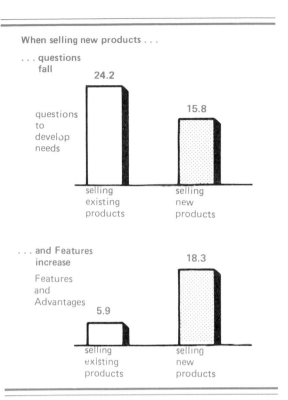

Figure 7.9 When selling new products, questions fall and features increase

product sales, when an important company in a medical market invited us to carry out an experiment with the launch of one of their new products. The product was a sophisticated, and expensive, piece of diagnostic equipment. It was clearly in the category of the larger sale. The machine was launched to most of the salesforce in the conventional way – a high-key presentation of its features and advantages by the product marketing team. But, for a small experimental group of salespeople, we were allowed to launch it differently. Instead of showing them the product and describing its features and advantages, we didn't even let them see what they would be selling. 'It's not important', we explained. 'What *is* important is that this machine is designed to solve problems for the doctors who use it.' We then listed the problems the machine solved and the needs it met. Finally, we had our group make a list of accounts where these problems could exist, together with the problem, implication and need-payoff questions they would ask when they visited those accounts. By launching the product in terms of the problems it solved and how to probe for them, we were able to shift our small group's attention away from the product and back to customer needs. The test that this was an effective strategy can be seen in the sales results. Our group averaged a 54 per cent higher level of sales than the rest of the sales force during the product's first year.

This research on new products also gave me an explanation for something which had puzzled me for many years. Some of the people with the best records for selling new products are the most cynical about product launches. I remember going to a product launch in Acapulco some years ago. The event was splendiferous. Big names from the entertainment world had been hired at unbelievable cost, the place swarmed with public relations people, media specialists, communications consultants and a variety of similarly expensive people. The salespeople, eagerly awaiting the great event, filed into the main hall to hear one of the most spectacular and costly feature dumps of the decade. I was depressed at the enormous expense my client had gone to in order to make the salesforce communicate the new product ineffectively, so I decided to wait outside until all the fuss and spectacle was over. As I sat by the pool I noticed two other people who had slipped out of the same presentation. Talking with them, I found that they were both very experienced high performers. 'It's just another product', said one, 'When the fuss dies down, I'll go back in and figure out which customers need it'. Clearly he wasn't going to fall into the trap of neglecting needs in favour of features and advantages.

Have you ever noticed how, just when the new product is proving a disappointment and the salesforce is losing its enthusiasm, sales suddenly start to improve? I recall exactly that happening when I was involved in the launch of a large new copying machine. At the time I thought it was curious that sales were terrible until the sales force stopped being excited by the new product. Then, at the point where everybody was beginning to say, 'This new machine isn't anything special', results took a dramatic turn for the better. I couldn't explain it because it seemed so much the opposite of common sense. You'd think that the machine would be most successful when it was new – with maximum salesforce enthusiasm and maximum competitive lead time. Now I know what was happening. As they became disillusioned, the attention of the salespeople turned away from the product and back to the customer.

There's a lesson here for anybody concerned with successful product launches. Several of our large multinational clients, on the basis of Huthwaite's research, now handle launches in a new way. Instead of giving features and advantages when they announce new products to the salesforce, they concentrate on explaining problems the product solves and questions which will uncover and develop those problems. It's proved a very successful method for speeding the growth curve of new product sales.

Techniques to help your selling

What are the main messages we've covered in this chapter which will help you demonstrate your capability more effectively in larger sales? I would pick out three main practical points.

1 Don't demonstrate capabilities too early

In smaller sales you can uncover a problem and jump straight in with advantages about how you can solve it. As we've seen, this doesn't work well in larger sales. It's important to develop explicit needs, using implication and need-payoff questions, before you offer solutions. Presenting capabilities too soon is one of the most common mistakes in large accounts. It's made worse because many customers will encourage you to present solutions in the absence of any information on needs. 'Just come and make a presentation about your product', they tell you, 'and *we'll* decide whether it fits our needs'. If you're forced to make presentations of features and advantages early in the selling cycle, always try to have a *minimum* of one pre-meeting with a key person in the account to uncover needs, so that your presentation includes at least some benefits.

2 Beware advantages

Most sales training, because it's based on models appropriate to smaller sales, encourages you to give advantage statements when you sell. And, to complicate the issue, the term they use for such statements is 'benefits'. Don't let previous training mislead you. Remember that, in larger sales, the powerful statements are those which show you can meet *explicit needs*. Don't fool yourself into thinking you're giving a lot of benefits if you're not uncovering and meeting those explicit needs.

3 Be careful with new products

Most of us give far too many features and advantages when we're selling new pro-

ducts. Don't let that happen to you. Instead, the first thing to ask yourself about any new product is 'What problems does it solve?' When you understand that, you can plan SPIN® questions to develop explicit needs. Try it. You'll be much more effective.

Answers to features, advantages, benefits knowledge test (pages 76-78)

1 *Feature:* Balanced voltage stabilisation is a fact about the system. The statement doesn't explain how stabilisation can be used or can help the customer.

2 *Advantage:* This statement shows how the feature in 1 can be used or can help the customer. Not a benefit because the customer hasn't expressed an explicit need for stabilisation.

3 *Advantage:* The statement shows how backup memory can be used or can help the customer, so it's more than just a feature. But, because there's no evidence that this customer has expressed an explicit need for backup memory, we can't call it a benefit.

4 *Feature:* Statements of cost, like this one are facts or data about the product, so we would classify them as features.

5 *Benefit:* In the previous statement, the customer has expressed an explicit need, 'I need to be able to read source data straight into memory'. In this statement the seller shows how the product meets that explicit need.

6 *Benefit:* Again, the buyer has stated an explicit need (an error rate less than 1 in 100 000). The seller shows that his product can easily meet the need.

7 *Advantage:* The seller shows another way in which having a low error rate

can be used or can help the customer. However, as the next customer statement shows, this doesn't meet a need.

8 *Feature:* A piece of data about the product.

9 *Feature:* Further product facts.

10 *Advantage:* The seller shows how the feature of time-based coding can be used to help the customer.

8

Preventing objections

During a visit to the training centre of a leading multinational company, I was invited to watch some sales training in progress. Instead of choosing the advanced systems selling class, as my hosts had perhaps expected, I asked instead if I could sit in on a typical basic-skills programme for new salespeople. Entering quietly at the back of the room, I looked around. The students all had that unnatural attentive cleanliness which goes with being new to sales. Their instructor, recently promoted from the field, was launching with great vigour into his favourite topic – objection-handling. You couldn't have imagined a more typical scene. It could have been day two of any basic sales training programme in any large company.

'The professional salesperson', began the instructor, *'welcomes* objections because they are a sign of customer interest. In fact, the more objections you get, the easier it will be for you to sell.' The class, duly impressed, wrote this down. Meanwhile I groaned behind my mandatory visitor's smile. Here was yet another new generation of salespeople at the receiving end of one of the most misleading myths in selling. Still, as a visitor it would have been improper for me to comment, so I continued to smile through an hour of objection-handling techniques until coffee break.

During coffee I talked with the instructor. 'Did you believe what you were saying in there?', I asked. 'That stuff about the more objections, the easier to sell?' 'Yes', he replied. 'If I didn't believe it, I wouldn't be teaching it.' I hesitated. Clearly the instructor and I had opposite views about objection-handling. It would have been easier to drop the subject, but he'd been kind enough to let me into his class – so I felt I owed him something in return. 'You've been a successful sales performer for several years, haven't you?' I asked. 'Yes', he replied with some pride. 'I've been with the company five years and I've made President's Club for the last three.' 'Look back at your own sales experience', I urged him. 'Five years ago, when you were new, did you receive more or fewer objections from your customers than you're getting now?' He thought for a moment. 'More, I guess', he replied. Then, as he remembered back, he added, 'You know, in the two years when I was new, I seemed to get objections all the time'. 'So', I asked, 'In those first two years when you were facing all those objections, did you have good sales figures?' 'No', he replied uncomfortably. 'In fact, my sales weren't too good until my third year with the company.' Pressing the point, I asked him, 'Then you did a lot better in that third year?' 'Yes', he said, 'that was the year I first made President's Club.' 'And how about objections?' I asked. 'It sounds as if you had *more* objections in your unsuccessful years. How does that tie in with what you said in class about the more objections, the more successful the call will be?' He considered the point for a while and replied, 'You're right, when I look back I faced many more objections when I was unsuccessful. Perhaps I'm teaching the wrong message'.

I had to admire him. Most people – given the astonishing human capacity for dismissing unwanted evidence – would have dodged the issue and held to their initial position. But the class was reconvening and I had to finish my tour of the facility, so I didn't have time to talk more with the instructor about objection-handling. If we'd had more time, I would have told him:

- objection-handling is a much less important skill than most training makes it out to be
- objections, contrary to common belief, are more often created by the seller than the customer
- in the average sales team, there is usually one salesperson who receives ten times as many objections per selling hour as another person in the same team.

- skilled people receive fewer objections because they have learned objection-prevention, not objection-handling.

To explain these findings, I'll have to go back to our discussion of features, advantages and benefits. You'll remember the definitions of these three behaviours and their links to success in sales of different sizes (Figure 8.1).

One of my colleagues, Linda Marsh, had been carrying out some correlation studies to check whether there were statistically significant links between each of these behaviours and the most probable responses they produced for customers. For example, when sellers use a lot of features in calls, do customers respond in a different way from their response in calls where *fewer* features are used? She discovered that features, advantages and benefits each produce a different behavioural response from customers (Figure 8.2).

BEHAVIOUR	DEFINITION	IMPACT	
		On Small Sales	On Larger Sales
FEATURES	describe facts, data, product characteristics	slightly positive	neutral or slightly negative
ADVANTAGES (Type A Benefits)	show how products, services or their features can be used or can help the customer	positive	slightly positive
BENEFITS (Type B Benefits)	show how products or services meet explicit needs expressed by the customer	very positive	very positive

Figure 8.1   Features, advantages and benefits

Seller behaviour	Most probable customer response
Features	price concerns
Advantages	objections
Benefits	support/approval

Figure 8.2   Most probable effect of features, advantages and benefits on customers

Features and price concerns

Customers are most likely to raise price concerns in calls where the seller gives lots of features. Why is this? It seems that the effect of features is to increase the customer's sensitivity to price. That's not necessarily a bad thing if you happen to be selling low-cost products that are rela-

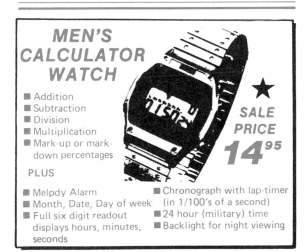

MEN'S CALCULATOR WATCH

- Addition
- Subtraction
- Division
- Multiplication
- Mark-up or mark-down percentages

PLUS

- Melody Alarm
- Month, Date, Day of week
- Full six digit readout displays hours, minutes, seconds
- Chronograph with lap-timer (in 1/100's of a second)
- 24 hour (military) time
- Backlight for night viewing

SALE PRICE 14⁹⁵

Figure 8.3   Offering features with low-cost products

tively rich in features. Consider the psychology of this advertisement (Figure 8.3).

This features-rich product is being sold in a way which works well with cheaper goods. You can imagine the television commercial. 'We give you multiplication, division, subtraction . . . and what do you think that's worth? Well, don't answer yet because you also get mark up and mark down percentages – which is something you don't usually find on watches ten times the price. And we also give you . . .' Throughout history, using features like this has helped to sell lower-priced goods. Why? Because features increase price sensitivity. By listing all the features, the customer comes to expect a higher price. When the product turns out to be much cheaper than its competition, the increased price sensitivity causes the buyer to feel extra-positive about the lower price tag.

I choose a watch example, rather than an industrial product, because there's something unique about watches. In no other market that I can think of, is there such an enormous price difference between competitors. In this next advertisement (Figure 8.4), the watch is twenty times as expensive as our earlier example.

Do you think you'd be more likely to buy this watch if there was a list of features down the side of the advertisement to help you? Not on your life! With top-of-the-market products, the price concern created by features will make people *less* likely to buy. A list of features would probably make you ask yourself questions about whether the expensive watch was worth it.

Too many features: a case study

The relationship between features and price concerns isn't just a theoretical point which applies only to advertisers. It has

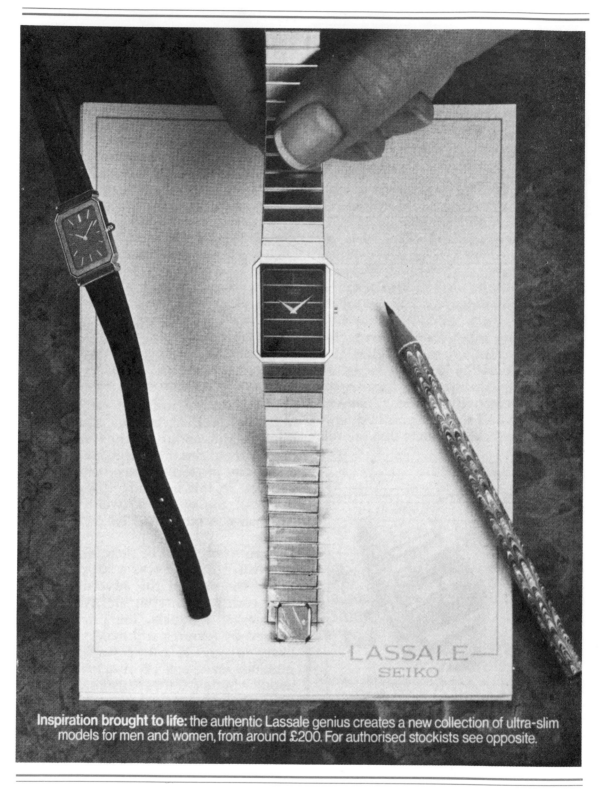

Inspiration brought to life: the authentic Lassale genius creates a new collection of ultra-slim models for men and women, from around £200. For authorised stockists see opposite.

Figure 8.4   Absence of features with high-cost products

clear implications for sales strategy. A major US-based multinational once called us in to help them with a problem. They had been facing tough Japanese competition in their primary marketplace, particularly at the lower end of their product range. The Japanese products were richly featured and, as you might expect, somewhat less expensive than the US company's own machines. As market share began to erode, the US company looked for alternatives to price cutting. One attractive possibility was to introduce a new product with more features which could compete directly with the Japanese machines. Such a machine would still be a little more expensive but, because of its features, would provide a much stronger marketplace offering.

But who would sell this new product? The company decided to recruit part of the sales force from the competition. After all, nobody knew as much about how to sell these richly-featured machines as salespeople who had been successful with their Japanese competitor. It seemed, on the face of it, a plausible strategy, recruiting experience for themselves while simultaneously weakening the competition by raiding their best people. They approached competitive salespeople who had been very successful selling the cheaper Japanese machines and succeeded in recruiting some of their competitor's top people.

Unfortunately, these new people's sales results were deeply disappointing. The competition's superstars performed no better than the existing salesforce. While trying to discover what was going wrong, I talked with several of the people recruited from competition and found them puzzled and dejected at their sudden fall from success. 'It's price,' they explained. 'The product's too expensive – we get price objections all the time'. And they were right. When we travelled with them on calls, we found that the number of price objections they received from customers was 30 per cent higher than for the rest of the sales force who were selling the same product. Why? We couldn't write it off as pure coincidence when two sections of a sales force selling an identical product received different levels of price objections from their customers.

The answer lay in their use of features. While selling for the cheaper competitor, these salespeople had developed a selling style very high in features. This was very successful because, as we've seen, features increase customer price concerns. But, because their product was cheaper, the price concern worked to their advantage. Now that they were selling for a more expensive competitor, the high level of features they were giving worked against them. Their features increased price concern and, because their product was more expensive, this turned customers towards the cheaper competitor. I presented our findings to the Sales Director for the division. As he wryly remarked, 'Right now, they seem to be doing a better job of selling for our competition than when our competition employed them'. How could we help? Not, I suggested, by teaching them how to handle price objections. That was just a symptom. It could be more effective to treat the *cause* and help these new people adopt a selling style more appropriate to a top-of-the-market product. So we retrained them in SPIN® questioning techniques so that they could use a high benefits style. As a result, their sales increased, price objections dropped and the price issues were soon forgotten.

Treating symptoms or treating causes?

Let me introduce a theme that I'll come back to several times in this chapter. Curing a selling problem, just like curing a disease, rests on finding and treating the *cause* rather than the symptoms. When I was nine years old I lived in

Borneo. A friend of my own age warned me that there was a typhoid epidemic in the village. All that either of us knew about typhoid was that it caused a burning fever. 'But I won't catch it,' he assured me, 'I'm eating a lot of ice cream to keep cool'. I followed his example – and caught typhoid from infected ice cream. One of the few things I remember clearly about my month seriously ill in hospital was my father explaining to me about the differences between symptoms – such as a high temperature – and causes, like the nasty little bacterium *Salmonella typhosa* which loves to lurk in ice cream. Perhaps this episode made me unduly sensitive to treating symptoms when you should be watching out for causes. But, just suppose we'd run a programme to teach those salespeople clever answers to price objections. Would we have achieved anything? I think not. The customer's price concern was just a symptom. The cause was giving too many features. Teaching objection-handling skills would do no more to prevent price concerns than eating ice cream would prevent typhoid.

Advantages and objections

Perhaps the most fascinating of the links which Linda Marsh found was the strong relationship between advantages and objections. You'll remember that advantages are statements which show how products or their features can be used or can help the customer – statements which many of us have been trained to call 'benefits'. In the last chapter we showed how advantages have a positive effect on small sales, but a much less positive effect when the sale grows larger. Linda's discovery offers a partial explanation. Advantages create objections – and that's one reason why they are poorly linked to success in the large scale.

To help understand the link between advantages and objections, consider this extract from an actual sales call. I've edited out references to the company and I've cut the length of some statements. Apart from that, this exact sequence of behaviours happened in a call we recorded in Dallas in September 1981. The product being sold is a word processor.

Seller: *(Problem question)* Does all this retyping waste time?

Buyer: *(Implied need)* Yes, some. But there's not so much of it here, not like in Fort Worth.

Seller: *(Advantage)* Here's where our word processors would be a very big help because they'd eliminate that retyping for you.

Buyer: *(Objection)* Look, we retype stuff, certainly. But you won't get me paying for fancy $15 000 machines just to cut down on some retyping.

Seller: *(Advantage)* I understand you, but the labour costs of retyping can climb out of sight. A big plus of word processors is that they save money by making your people more efficient.

Buyer: *(Objection)* We're very efficient right now – and if I wanted to do better on efficiency I can think of sixteen ways without new word processors. I've two xxx word processors there in the back office. Nobody really knows how to use them. They give trouble, just trouble.

Seller: *(Problem question)* Those xxx machines are hard for your people to use?

Buyer: *(Implied need)* Yes, it's quicker to type it out by hand – doing it the old way.

Seller: *(Advantage)* We really can help you there. Our yyy machines use a screen, so people can see exactly what they're doing. That's a lot better than your old xxx's where you've got to remember things like format codes

– which we prompt automatically, so that our machines can be used much more easily.

Buyer: *(Objection)* Do you know something? Some of the ladies working here get uptight about a typewriter with a correcting ribbon. Screen? It would just totally confuse them. I'd end up with more mistakes than I'm getting now.

Seller: *(Problem question)* You're getting too many mistakes?

Seller: *(Implied need)* Some. Well, no more than most offices, but more than I like.

Seller: *(Advantage)* Tests show that with the full screen editing and error correction we offer, your error rates would drop by more than 20 per cent if you used our machines.

Buyer: *(Objection)* Yes . . . but it's not worth all that just to get rid of a few typo's . . .

What's happened here? The first thing you'll notice is that every advantage is followed by an objection. Of course, I've chosen this extract to illustrate my point – objections don't *always* follow advantages the way they do in the example I've picked here. Sometimes the seller will use an advantage which brings a favourable response from the customer. But, from our research, objections are a more likely response than any other buyer behaviour.

The next thing to notice about this example is the characteristic sequence of behaviours: problem question → implied need → objection. We found this sequence happening over and over again in unsuccessful calls. Let's look more closely at what's going on (Figure 8.5).

As you can see, the fundamental problem which is causing the objection is that the seller offered a solution before building up the need. The buyer doesn't feel that the problem has enough *value* to merit such an expensive solution. Consequently, when the seller gives the advantage, the buyer raises an objection.

This explains why advantages have a more positive effect in small sales. If the word processor had cost $15 instead of $15 000, the buyer would probably have reacted differently. It's certainly worth $15 to eliminate retyping. But $15 000? That's a different matter.

Back to symptoms and causes

How would you help the seller in our example? It's tempting to suggest that because she is receiving so many objections, what she needs is better objection-handling skills. So, for example, we could teach her principles of objection-handling – the classic techniques of acknowledging, rephrasing and answering. Or we could give her *specific* help with the common objections customers raise, by showing her what to say when customers raise typical objections like:

'Your word processors are too expensive'
'Word processors are hard to use'
'My people would be resistant to word processors'
'Word processors are more trouble than they're worth'

Either of these options would help her handle future objections better. But are we treating the symptoms or the cause? In each case, in the example, the objection arose because the seller hadn't built sufficient *value* before offering solutions. Teaching her how to handle objections treats the symptom but it doesn't alter the cause. The fundamental selling disease – jumping in too soon with solutions – remains malignant and untreated.

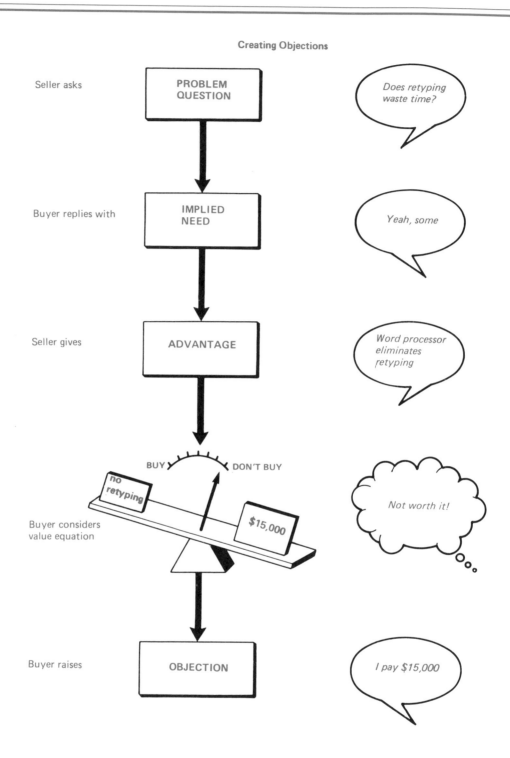

Figure 8.5   Creating objections

The cure

If objection-handling just treats a symptom, how would we set about a complete cure? That's where the SPIN® model comes in. By teaching her to probe in a way which builds *value* we can prevent the objection from arising in the first place. Let me show you what I mean, using the final objection in the example. First let's examine why the customer raised the objection in the first place.

Seller: *(Problem question)* You're getting too many mistakes?

Buyer: *(Implied need)* Some. Well, no more than most offices, but more than I like.

Seller: *(Advantage)* Tests show that with the full screen editing and error correction we offer, your error rates would drop by more than 20 per cent if you used our machines.

Buyer: *(Objection)* Yes . . . but it's not worth all that hassle just to get rid of a few typo's . . .

The customer has raised the objection because he doesn't perceive sufficient *value* from reducing error rate. If you could draw a value-equation diagram to show what was going on in the customer's mind, it would probably look like this (Figure 8.6).

Hassle greatly outweighs the value of eliminating a few mistakes, so the customer makes a negative judgement and raises an objection. Even the best objection-handling skills can't alter the fact that the seller has offered a solution without first building value. Let's look at how a more skilled person would handle the same situation:

Seller: *(Problem question)* You're getting too many mistakes?

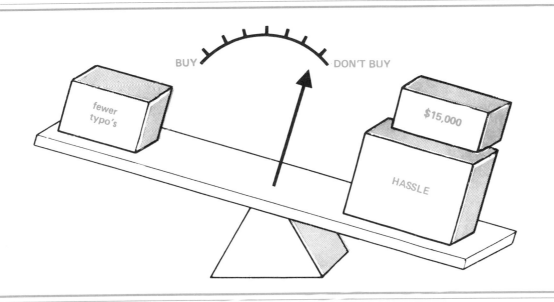

Figure 8.6   Value equation: cost of solution outweighs problem

Buyer: (*Implied need*) Some. Well, no more than most offices, but more than I would like.

Seller: (*Implication question*) You say 'more than you'd like'; does that mean that some of those mistakes are causing you difficulties in documents you send out to clients?

Buyer: Sometimes that's happened, but not often because I proof-read all important documents carefully before I send them out.

Seller: (*Implication question*) Doesn't that take up a lot of your time?

Buyer: Too much. But it's better than letting a document out with a mistake – particularly if it's a mistake in the figures that go out to a client.

Seller: (*Implication question*) Why would that be? Are you saying that a mistake in the figures would lead to more serious consequences with clients than a mistake in the text.

Buyer: Oh yes. We could lose a bid, or commit ourselves to an uneconomic contract – or even just come across to clients as sloppy. People judge you on things like that. That's why it's worth a couple of hours a day proof-reading when there's other things I should be doing.

Seller: (*Need-payoff question*) Suppose you didn't have to spend that time proof-reading, what could you do with the time you saved?

Buyer: Well, I could give some time to training my office people.

Seller: (*Need-payoff question*) And that training would lead to improved productivity?

Buyer: Oh, very much. At the moment, you see, people don't know how to use some of the equipment here – that graph plotter for example – so they have to wait until I'm free to do it.

Seller: (*Implication question*) So the time you're spending in proofing also forces you to become a bottleneck for other people's work?

Buyer: Yes, I'm badly overloaded.

Seller: (*Need-payoff question*) Then anything which reduced the time you're spending in proofing wouldn't just help you, it would also help the productivity of others?

Buyer: Right.

Seller: (*Need-payoff question*) I can see how by reducing proof-reading you could ease the present bottleneck – is there any other way that having fewer mistakes in documents would help you?

Buyer: Sure. People here hate retyping. It might be a plus in terms of their motivation if fewer mistakes meant less time spent in retyping.

Seller: (*Need-payoff question*) And presumably less time in retyping would also bring cost savings?

Buyer: You're right. And that's something I need to do.

Seller: (*Summarising*) So it seems that the present level of mistakes is leading to expensive retyping, which creates a motivation problem with your people. If mistakes, particularly in figures, get out to your clients it can be very damaging. You're trying to prevent that at the moment by spending two hours a day proofing all key documents. But that's turning you into a bottleneck, reducing everyone's productivity and preventing you from putting time into training your staff.

Buyer: When you put it that way, those mistakes in documents are really hurting us. We can't just ignore the problem – I've got to do something about it.

Seller: (*Benefit*) Then let me show you how our word processor would help you cut mistakes and reduce proofing . . .

If we were to re-examine the customer's value equation (Figure 8.7), what would we find?

Now the cost and hassle are more than counterbalanced by the *value* which the seller has created through the use of implication and need-payoff questions. It's a much more effective piece of selling because we've attacked the *cause* of the objection. As a result, the objection doesn't even arise. Objection prevention turns out to be a superior strategy to objection handling.

Objection prevention : a case study

I can imagine people reading this and saying to themselves, 'Yes, it all sounds very plausible when Rackham's making up examples which suit his case, but I'm not sure that it holds up in the real world'. As a further piece of evidence I'd like to share with you one of the most fascinating little investigations I was ever involved with.

The company was a well-known high-tech corporation whose personnel research staff had been investigating sales behaviour in one of their divisions based in the southern United States. We had encouraged them to use the behaviour analysis method of counting how often key seller and customer behaviours occurred during sales calls. They had come up with a curious finding. The average sales team in the division consisted of eight salespeople. Now, purely in terms of statistical probabilities, you'd expect that those eight people, each selling the same product to the same size of customer and

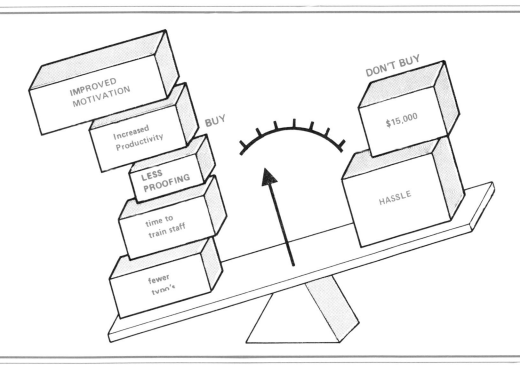

Figure 8.7   Value equation: problem now outweighs cost of solution

with the same competitors, would each face approximately the same number of objections per selling hour. Not so. There was an enormous difference in the number of objections faced by individual sales people. In the average team they often found one salesperson having to face *ten times* as many objections per selling hour as other people from the same team.

The company didn't know about our work on the links between advantages and objections. Naturally, they drew the obvious conclusion: these people who were receiving so many objections must need training in objection-handling. They asked us for advice. One quick look at their data told us what we needed to know. We picked the behaviour analysis figures for ten people who were each receiving very high numbers of objections and who were clearly candidates for objection-handling training. In all ten cases, these people were higher than average in the numbers of advantages they used in their calls.

I persuaded the company to try a bold experiment. 'What I'd like to do,' I explained, 'is to train these people in objection-*prevention*. I think we can design a programme which doesn't even mention the word 'objection', but which will do more for these people than the best objection-handling training ever could.' They agreed. We chose 8 sales-people who – from the behaviour analysis figures – had each received an unusually high level of objections from customers. As we'd promised, our training didn't say anything at all about objections or objection-handling. Instead we taught the eight people to develop explicit needs with the SPIN® model and then to offer benefits.

After the training, the company's researchers went out with the eight to count the number of objections they were now receiving in calls. The average number of objections per selling hour had fallen by

55 per cent. I'd draw two conclusions from this little study:

- It's confirmation that the best way to handle objections is through prevention. Treat the cause and not the symptom.
- Notice that our training didn't prevent objections *completely*.

There always will be objections which arise because the customer has needs your product can't meet, or a competitor has a clear product superiority. These 'true' objections are facts of life and no objection prevention techniques can do anything to stop them from being raised. However, what we were able to show in this case was that objections can be cut by more than half through using the SPIN® behaviours to build value.

The sales training approach to objections

Sales training actually teaches people to *create* objections, then teaches them techniques for handling the objections they've inadvertently created. That's because the selling skills models in every major sales training programme we've reviewed have been based on the small sale. As we've seen, in small sales a high level of advantages can be successful because there's less need to build value before offering solutions. But in larger sales advantages don't have that positive impact. It's important to remember that we're using the term 'advantage' to cover any statement which shows how your product or service can be used or can help the customer – in other words, what we're calling an advantage is what most sales training calls a benefit.

It's my hope, as training designers begin to understand that larger sales need different skills, that we'll see an end to the kind of training which encourages salespeople to give a lot of advantages. The heavy use of advantages – which is what most training recommends – is the cause of more than half the objections which customers raise. But are objections necessarily bad? Some sales training programmes, and many sales trainers like the instructor I described at the start of this chapter, teach that objections are positively linked to success and the more you get the better. If that's true, then preventing objections could actually *hurt* your selling. What does the evidence tell us? We carried out a study to find out whether objections were really 'sales opportunities in disguise', as one training programme put it. We counted the number of objections raised by customers in a sample of 694 calls collected from an international sample in a large business machines corporation (see Figure 8.8).

As you can see, the higher the percentage of objections in the customer's behaviour, the less likely that the call will succeed. If objections are sales opportunities in disguise, then this study suggests that their disguise must have been created by a master in camouflage. No, make no mistake about it, the more objections you get in a call, the less likely you are to be successful. It's a comforting myth for trainers to tell inexperienced salespeople that professionals welcome objections as a sign of customer interest. But in reality an objection is a barrier between you and your customer. However skilfully you dismantle that barrier through objection-handling, it would be wiser not to have created it in the first place.

Benefits and support/approval

The most positive relationship to emerge from Linda Marsh's study of features, advantages and benefits was the strong link between giving benefits and receiving expressions of approval or support

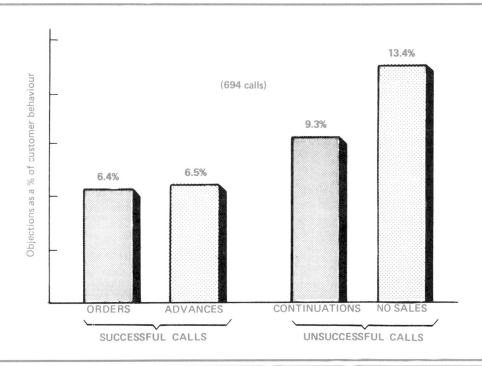

Figure 8.8 Objection levels and call success

from customers. The more benefits sellers gave, the more approving statements their customers made. This isn't a surprising finding. After all, benefits – as we define them – involve showing how you can meet an explicit need which the customer has expressed. Unless the customer first says, 'I want it', you can't give a benefit. It's no wonder that customers are most likely to express approval when you show you can give them something they want.

Objection handling versus objection prevention

At its most basic, what I've suggested in this chapter is that the old objection-*handling* strategies, which encourage the seller to give advantages, are much less successful in the larger sale than objection-*prevention* strategies, where the seller first develops value using implication and need-payoff questions before offering capabilities (Figure 8.9).

When I was new to selling I thought that, next to closing, objection-handling skills were the most crucial to sales success. Looking back, I can now see that my concern was motivated by the large number of objections I was facing from my customers. I didn't ask myself what caused the objections – just that there were lots of them, so I'd better improve my objection-handling. I now understand that the majority of objections I faced were only a symptom caused by poor selling. By improving my probing skills I've become more successful at objection-prevention – and that's certainly helped me sell more successfully. I still get objections, of course – in selling there will always be potential for a genuine mismatch between customer needs and what a seller can offer. So objection-handling skills will always have a part to play in my calls. But the reason I sell better now isn't

better objection-handling skills, it's that I'm less likely to create unnecessary objections.

Techniques to help your selling

If you're receiving more objections from customers than you'd like, think about which is symptom and which is cause. Could it be that objections are just a symptom you've caused by offering your solutions too soon in the call? Try putting extra effort into effective needs development, using implication and need-payoff questions. If you can build the *value* of your solutions, then you're much less likely to face objections. As many hundreds of salespeople we've trained will testify, good questioning skills will do more to help you with objections than any objection-handling techniques ever could.

Of course, you'll always get *some* objections, especially when your product doesn't meet a customer's needs. However, here are two sure signs which tell you you're getting unnecessary objections which can be prevented by better questioning:

- *Objections early in the call*
  Customers rarely object to questions – unless you've found a particularly offensive way to ask them. Most objections are to solutions which don't fit needs. If you're getting a lot of objections early in the call, it probably means that instead of asking questions you've been prematurely offering solutions and capabilities. The cure is simple enough – don't talk about solutions until you've asked enough questions to develop strong needs.

- *Objections about value*
  If most of the objections you receive raise doubts about the *value* of what

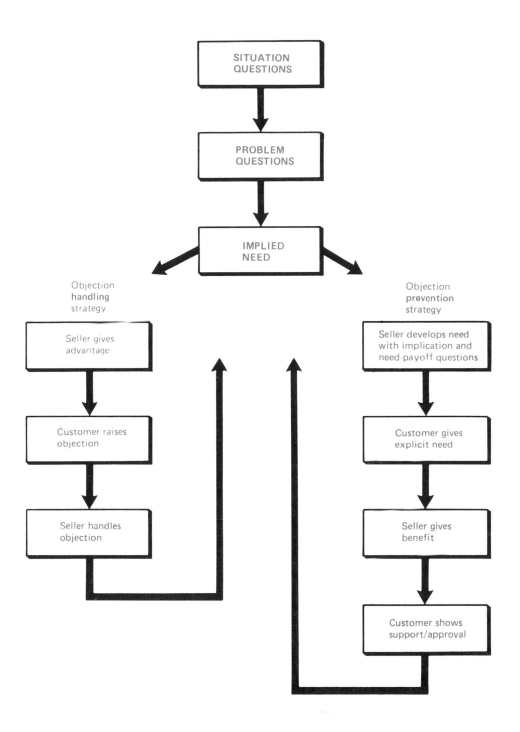

Figure 8.9   Objection handling or objection prevention?

you offer, then there's a good chance that you're not developing needs strongly enough. Typical objections would be, 'It's too expensive', 'I don't think it's worth the trouble of changing from our existing supplier' or 'We're happy with our existing system'. In cases like these, customer objections tell you that you haven't succeeded in building a strong need. The solution lies in better needs development not in objection handling. Particularly if you're getting a lot of price objections, cut down on the use of features and, instead, concentrate on asking problem, implication and need-payoff questions.

9

Preliminaries: opening the call

In this chapter I want to examine preliminaries more closely. To be honest, the Huthwaite research team didn't find the preliminaries stage of the call very exciting when compared with the central areas of investigating and demonstrating capability. That's perhaps our personal bias, and it meant we did much less research in this area than in the other three stages. Nevertheless, even the limited data we did collect showed that successful ways of opening the call in a small sale are different from those which work best as the size of sale increases (Figure 9.1).

Preliminaries

How important is the warming-up stage of the call? In our research on preliminaries we were trying to answer a number of questions such as:

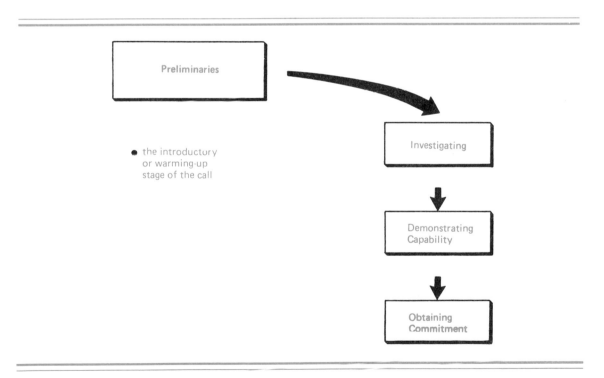

Figure 9.1   Preliminaries

- Is it true that first impressions made in a sales call are crucial to its success?
- Do the openings which work in smaller sales work equally well in larger ones?
- Is there one particular way to open a call which is better than others?

There's evidence to suggest that people notice far less in the early stages of an interaction than we may imagine. Many of the older books on selling emphasise the importance of a smart appearance and suggest that first impressions will make or break the sale. Most recent research suggests that initial appearances are far less important than these older writers have claimed. That's not to say that it pays to be scruffy or unpresentable. A reasonable standard of dress is probably sensible. But don't believe that tiny details will make a big difference to your sales success in the preliminaries stage of the sale. As we've seen, far more important, and more durable impressions are made during the investigating stage. In the early stages of an interaction with another person, we're usually so overloaded with information that we either don't notice, or we quickly forget, some quite obvious things. How often have you been introduced to someone and, ten seconds later, you've forgotten their name? Why should you forget something as important as a name? Because your mind is full of other things, such as what you're going to say next. You literally don't have room for all the detail available to you. Many potential important impressions get crowded out in the opening minutes of a meeting.

It's hard to get accurate data on the importance of first impressions. But let me give you my personal opinion from watching the opening to many hundreds of sales calls. Over and over again I've seen successful calls which started in a nondescript or even awkward manner. And I've seen tremendously smooth openings lead nowhere. Over the years I've come to doubt the importance of first impressions during the preliminary stage of the call. I no longer believe that first impressions can make or break your sales success in larger sales. It may be that in very small sales, such things as dress or opening words do matter. A friend of mine was raising money for a charity by door-to-door selling of Christmas cards. I believe him when he claims that there was a direct relationship between how his volunteers dressed and how much they sold. One day, he told me, he insisted that everyone wear their best clothes. Sales went up by 20 per cent. But don't expect a smart suit and a good opening sentence to add 20 per cent to your sales volume if you're in major account selling.

The multi-call sale

So far, I've written about preliminaries in the larger sale as though I'm talking about a first meeting with a new customer. I've done that for the sake of simplicity, although we must recognise that most larger sales involve several calls and are likely to be with customers where there's already an established relationship. With some major account groups I've known, less than 5 per cent of their calls have been first time meetings with new customers. The factors which influence preliminaries in the multi-call sale haven't, to my knowledge, been researched by anyone. It seems likely that with existing customers and also with new customers as the selling cycle progresses, the impact of preliminaries gets less because the relationship has become well established. But nobody knows for sure, and I'd prefer to avoid speculation. Consequently, I'm going to concentrate on areas where some data exists. Although we don't have research into the impact of preliminaries across a whole sales cycle, we *do* have information about opening first calls on new customers in both large and small sales.

Opening the smaller sale

Since the 1920s salespeople have been taught that there are two successful ways to open a call.

- *Relate to the buyer's personal interests*
  The conventional sales wisdom says that if you can somehow tap in to an area of personal interest, then you can form a relationship more quickly and the call will be more successful. So, for example, if your buyer has a photograph of children on the desk, then discuss family interests; if there's a golf trophy in the office, then talk golf.

- *Making an opening benefit statement*
  Begin with some dramatic statement about the benefits your product can offer. So, for example, you might say, 'Ms Customer, in today's marketplace productivity is the concern of key executives like yourself – and our product will contribute to *your* productivity'.

Our evidence suggests that, while these two methods might be successful in smaller sales, there's little to show that they help when the sale is larger. Let's review our evidence.

Relating to personal interests

In one of Huthwaite's early studies, carried out in part of the Imperial Group, we were trying to establish whether salespeople who built good relationships would, as a result, make more sales. We found that sellers who dealt successfully with small retail outlets in rural areas seemed to rely heavily on personal factors in their selling. We measured the number of times each seller referred to some fact or incident which was related to the customer's personal life. For example, the seller might ask, 'How's Ann enjoying her riding lessons?' or 'Is Joe's leg better yet?' In rural areas, where the size of sale was small, successful sellers used more of these personal references than those who were less successful. So we could safely conclude that the old advice is right. If you can relate to points of personal interest, then it will help your selling.

But it was a different story in the large urban stores, where the average sale was more than five times the size. We found no relationship between success and reference to personal issues. It seemed that relating to the buyer's personal interests might be a less effective technique in larger sales. I wasn't particularly satisfied with this study. For a number of technical reasons we had to be cautious about our interpretation. For example, the rural salespeople generally had longer tenure and a lower turnover rate. That meant they were in the job longer and so had more opportunity to find out personal things about their customers. The rural customers themselves were less busy than their large urban counterparts, so they had more time to talk.

Nevertheless, this study raised some questions. Possibly, in the 1920s when the theory was first put forward, it was true that people bought from those they related to personally; friends did business with friends. But, even in the mere fifteen years I've been studying selling, I've noticed a distinct change. Fifteen years ago buyers would tell me, 'I buy from Fred because I like him'. Now I'm much more likely to hear, 'I like Fred, but I buy from his competition because they're cheaper'. It seems that personal loyalty is no longer an adequate basis for doing business.

The yacht which increased productivity

There's another reason why it may not be successful to open a call around a personal point. I once worked with the central purchasing group of British Petroleum. One of the buyers had, on the wall of his office, a picture of a racing yacht. 'I keep it there because it improves my efficiency', he told me. Puzzled, I asked him to explain. 'I get salespeople coming in here every day', he explained, 'wasting my time by talking about a lot of non-business issues. Obviously they're fishing for some personal area which will catch my interest. But I'm a busy professional purchaser – and I couldn't get through the day if I wasted time on conversation which isn't directly business-related. So I use the picture to increase my productivity. When new sales reps visit me for the first time they usually say, "What a beautiful picture. You must really enjoy sailing." I reply, "I hate sailing. That picture's there to remind me how much time gets wasted out on the water. Now, what did you want to see me about?" '

Perhaps that's an extreme case, but I've heard many other professional buyers complain about salespeople who try to open calls by cultivating areas of personal interest. The last thing a busy buyer wants is to tell the tenth seller of the day all about his last game of golf. The more senior the person you're selling to, the more they feel their time is at a premium, and the more impatience you're likely to generate if you dwell on non-business areas. And there's another reason. Many buyers become suspicious of people who begin by raising areas of personal interest. They feel that the seller's motives aren't genuine and that it's an attempt to manipulate them.

I'm not saying that you should never begin a sales call by talking about a buyers personal interests. Sometimes, particularly if the buyer takes the lead in raising an area, it's the right thing to do. And, as we've seen, in smaller sales there can be an overall positive impact on sales success from raising personal issues. But, as a general piece of advice, I'd suggest that you're careful not to over-use this method in larger sales.

106

The opening benefit statement

Many sales training programmes teach that the most effective way to begin the call is to make an opening benefit statement to catch the buyer's interest with some potential benefit of your product or service. So I might say, 'Mr Wilson, for a busy executive like yourself, I know that time is money. And I'm sure you waste a lot of time looking up telephone numbers and dialling calls. With the Rackham Autodialler I could help save some of that time for you'. If it's well done, then an opening benefit statement can sound positive and businesslike. But is it an effective way to open calls?

Although the idea of the opening benefit statement is quite old – I've been able to trace it back thirty years and it might even go back further than that – its great popularity as an opening was brought about by the Xerox Learning System programme, *Professional Selling Skills*. This programme was very widely used, and claimed that research showed calls were more likely to be successful if they started this way – using, as they called it, an *initial benefit statement*. I haven't seen the detailed research and so I can't comment on its validity. But I do know that the investigation on which the programme was based took place in the pharmaceutical industry – where the average call length was a mere 6 minutes. If you've only 6 minutes of buyer time, then I could certainly see why you would need a punchy way to get straight into the substance of your call.

But would the same be true in larger sales, where the average individual call length is 40 minutes? That's what Huthwaite set out to investigate. We watched just over three hundred calls, noting whether or not the seller used an opening benefit statement. Then, using the procedure described in chapter one, we divided the calls into those which succeeded and those which failed. If opening benefit statements made calls more successful, as the PSS programme claimed, then we should expect to find that the calls which failed had fewer opening benefit statements than the calls which succeeded. That's not what we found. In our studies there was no relationship, one way or another, between the use of opening benefit statements and the success of the call.

Why should a useful-sounding method, like the opening benefit statement, not be related to success in some way? We decided to look more closely.

What we found was this. The most effective salespeople we studied opened each call in a different way. Sometimes they might use an opening benefit statement, but frequently they would use some other starting point. Less effective people were the ones who tended to open each call in the same way. So those sellers who began *every* call with an opening benefit statement were likely to be less successful than those who just used the technique occasionally.

Larger sales mean multiple calls – often several on the same customer, so it's particularly important not to use a standard opening more than once with the same person. I can recall how impressed I was with a salesperson from an office products company when he first called on me. He began with a classic opening benefit statement, 'Mr Rackham, you're a busy executive and I'm sure you're wondering whether it's worth 15 minutes of your time to talk to me. But if, as a result of that 15 minutes, you could save your company several thousand dollars, I'm sure you'd agree that it would be time well spent . . .'. So I gave him 15 minutes and was sufficiently impressed with his product to invite him back the following week to talk to us again. At the next meeting, with my office manager present, he began, 'Mr Rackham, I know you're busy, but if I could use 15 minutes of your

time to show you how I could save your company thousands of dollars . . .'. The very opening which had made such a positive impression first time round, now sounded mechanical and irritating.

There's another reason why the opening benefit statement may be ineffective. Successful salespeople talk about their products or services late in the sales call. We've seen that less-successful people begin talking products and solutions very much earlier in the call. I remind you of that point here because it raises a danger from the use of opening benefit statements. Take this simple example:

Seller: (*Using opening benefit statement*)Mr Buzzard, we at Big Co know how important it is to produce professional looking documents in a business like yours. That's why we invented the Executype typewriter. Using a special new system, the Executype gives a far finer finish to your documents than you can get from conventional word processors.

Buyer: (*Asking the questions*) Oh. Does it use a daisywheel?

Seller: (*Drawn into giving product details*) No. It's an inkjet process.

Buyer: (*Still asking the questions*) Inkjet? that must be very expensive, Ms Simpson, what does it cost?

Seller: (*Forced into a price issue early in the call*) Er . . . well, it *is* a little more expensive than conventional methods but it's also got . . .

What's happened here? By making an opening benefit statement the seller has been trapped in two ways. She has:

- been forced to talk about product details too early in the sale, before she's had an opportunity to build value using SPIN® questions.
- allowed the *buyer* to ask questions and therefore to take control of the discussion.

107

Neither of these traps is irreversible and, if she's smart, Ms Simpson will recover the call, take over the questioning role from the buyer and turn attention away from the product and back towards the customer's need. But, at the very least, this isn't a good way to begin the sale. Yet I've personally seen many calls which have started this way because the seller has used an opening benefit statement.

A strategy for opening the call

Everything you've read so far is negative – it's about how not to handle the preliminaries stage of the call. Let's turn our attention to the positives. What does Huthwaite's research recommend as the best way to open calls? Obviously, as I've suggested, variety is important. There isn't one best opening technique. But there *is* a framework which successful people use.

Let's examine the objective of the preliminaries stage of the call. What's the purpose of your opening? At its very simplest, what you're trying to do is to get the customer's consent to move on to the next phase – the investigating stage. You want customers to agree that it's legitimate for you to ask them some questions. In order to do that, a good opening must establish:

- who you are
- why you're there (but not through giving product details)
- your right to ask questions.

Sometimes this can be accomplished very simply. I could say, for example, 'Hello, Ms Blunt. I'm Neil Rackham from Huthwaite. We're sales training consultants. Would it be okay if I asked you some questions about your present sales training?' In a less-simple opening it might take more time to achieve the same end and require something more like:

Rackham: Hello, Mr Badger. I'm pleased to meet you. I'm Neil Rackham from Huthwaite (*establishing who I am*).

Badger: You wanted to talk to me about sales training or something?

Rackham: Yes (*establishing why I'm here*).

Badger: Aren't you the people who produced the SPIN® programme?

Rackham: Yes, that's one of our products – and if you agree, I'd like to talk to you about whether it might be a useful programme for you here in Hard Co (*further establishing why I'm here*).

Badger: I very much doubt it. We've designed our own training internally and we're very satisfied with it.

Rackham: Then it's possible that the SPIN® programme isn't what you need. Would you mind if I check that out by asking you a few questions about your present programme? (*establishing the right to ask questions*).

Obviously there are many different ways to open, but the common factor of most good openings is that they lead the customer to agree that you should ask questions. In doing so, a good opening avoids getting into detailed discussion of your products or services. Early in the call, you want to establish your role as the seeker of information and the buyer's role as the giver.

. . . and a summary

I set out to answer three questions about the preliminaries stage of a sales call.

1 *Is it true that the first couple of minutes of a sales call are crucial to its success?*
   Our answer was that there's some evidence in small sales that this might be true, but there's little to suggest that it's true in larger sales.

2 *Do the openings which work in smaller*

sales work equally well in larger ones?
We showed how the two traditional openings of relating to the buyer's personal interest and making an opening benefit statement were more likely to be successful in small sales than in large.

3 *Is there one particular way to open the call which is better than others?*
We fould that successful people used a wide variety of openings. Less-successful people tended to have one preferred way to open the call. But a common factor among most successful openings was that they established who the seller was, why the seller was there and the right to answer questions.

Techniques to help your selling

Preliminaries, as we've seen, don't play a crucial role in the larger sale. The most important test of whether you're handling preliminaries effectively is whether your customers are generally happy to move ahead and answer your questions. If so, then you're probably handling this stage of the call acceptably. Don't worry about appearing smooth and polished – some of the best salespeople we've studied have seemed nervous, self-conscious or hesitant in the early minutes of the call.

Do worry, however, about how long the preliminaries stage takes you. It's not the most productive part of the call for you or for the customer. A common mistake, particularly for inexperienced salespeople, is spending too long on pleasantries. As a result the call runs short of time – the customer has to stop just when you're getting to a critical point. If you find that your calls often run out of time, it's worth asking yourself whether you're getting down to business quickly enough. While there's no exact measure for how long it

should take to open a call, I'd be worried by anyone who consistently spent more than 20 per cent of the call time on preliminaries. Don't feel that you'll offend customers by getting down to business quickly. A complaint I frequently hear from senior executives and professional buyers is that salespeople waste their time with idle chatter. I don't think I've ever heard the complaint that a salesperson gets too quickly down to business.

Talking solutions too soon

One of the most common faults in selling is talking about your solutions and capabilities too early in the call. As we've seen in previous chapters, offering solutions too soon causes objections and greatly reduces the chances that the call will succeed. How often do you find yourself discussing your products, services or solutions with the customer during the first half of the call? If it happens frequently then it may be a sign that you're not handling preliminaries effectively. If, in your case, it's usually the customer who is asking the questions and you're in the role of providing facts and explanations, then it's likely you've not sufficiently established your role as a questioner during the preliminaries. Ask yourself whether your call opening establishes that *you* should be asking the questions. If not, then change the way you open calls so that the customer accepts that you'll be asking some questions before you talk about the capabilities you can offer.

Finally, remember that preliminaries aren't the most important part of the call. Often, when I've been travelling with salespeople, I've noticed that they waste time before a call worrying about how they should open it when they could be using that time far more effectively to plan some questions instead.

10

Obtaining commitment: closing the sale

When we were researching preliminaries, there was almost nothing written about call opening and nowhere we could go for advice. Not so at the other end of the sale. The final stage, obtaining commitment, was an area where more had been written than I'd have imagined possible. Several years ago, before the days when you could get a computer to do the work for you, I spent a couple of weeks in the library searching for all I could find about closing the sale. I ploughed through more than three hundred references. Every book on selling had at least one chapter on closing. Some, like '101 Sure Fire Ways To Irresistibly Close *Any* Sale', had, as the author modestly put it, 'a lifetime's experience of closing success packed into a mere three hours of reading'.

I was fascinated. Here were magic answers to the problems of generating business. The closes I read about included the good old standard techniques which every seller knows, such as:

Assumptive closes: assuming the sale has already been made by, for example, asking 'where would you like it delivered?' before the customer has agreed to buy.

Alternative closes: for example, 'Would you prefer delivery on Tuesday or Thursday?' again before the customer has made a purchasing decision.

Standing-room-only closes: for example, 'If you can't make a decision right now, I'll have to offer it to another customer who's pressing to buy it'.

Last-chance closes: for example, 'The price goes up next week, so unless you buy now . . .'.

Order blank closes: filling in the customer's answers on an order form, even though the buyer has not indicated willingness to make a buying decision.

In addition to these bread-and-butter techniques, I found a whole encyclopedia of more exotic closes, such as the sharp angle, Ben Franklin, puppy dog, Colombo and double-reverse whammo. My initial research uncovered literally hundreds of closes and, in the intervening years, I'm sure that new closes have continued to appear with impressive regularity. Just last month I was reading an airline magazine which mentioned the banana close – a new one for me – and on the same day my junk mail contained a hard-to-resist invitation to learn more about the half-open close – a hidden secret of sales success which I'd somehow missed.

No other area of selling skill is as popular as closing. That's true however you measure it, whether by number of words written, number of instructional hours or number of feet of training films endured by each new generation of salespeople. I was once told by a leading editor that he wouldn't publish any book on selling unless it had the word 'closing' in the title. In surveys of sales managers, asking them what skill they would most like to increase in their people, closing has always emerged a clear winner. So there seems widespread support for the old selling proverb, 'The ABC of selling is Always Be Closing'. In this chapter I'm going to be asking:

● How many of these closing techniques actually work?
● In larger sales, how do factors such as price and buyer sophistication influence the success of closing?

What is closing?

Unfortunately, very few of the writers who have so persuasively filled volumes on how to close have defined the term 'closing'. Crissy and Kaplan called it, 'the tactics used by the salesman to induce purchase or acceptance of the proposition'. As a researcher, I find that definition too broad. We needed a more limited, and more precise, way to define a closing behaviour. Closing, in our studies, was

> A behaviour used by the seller which implies or invites a commitment, so that the buyer's next statement accepts or denies commitment.

In more digestible English, a close is anything which puts the customer in a position which involves some kind of commitment. This definition covers the whole spectrum from simply 'asking for the order' to using the wildly complex 'twelve-step-staircase' technique.

The consensus on closing

Closing is a fertile area for sales gurus. Before I review Huthwaite's studies, let me introduce some of the points which other experts have made. J. Douglas Edwards, called by his disciples 'the father of closing', suggests that, on average, successful sellers close on their fifth attempt and the more closing techniques they use, the more successful they are likely to be. Alan Schoonmaker is even more specific about the success of closing. He too claims that research shows successful sellers close more often and use more types of closes. And like J. Douglas Edwards, he favours the magic number five, saying, 'you haven't done your job if you quit without asking for the order at least five times'. I paid particular attention to Schoonmaker because, at the time, I was developing a training programme on the larger sale for IBM and I knew that he was working on a similar programme for one of their competitors.

P. Lund, in the book *Compelling Selling*, advises you to close whenever possible – 'even when you're miles away from the order'. Another popular writer, Mauser, is more restrained, advising you to have a considerable number of closing techniques at your disposal so that if one fails, another can be used 'until it is hoped one eventually hits the mark'. I could go on, but I think I've made the point. The consensus among writers on selling seems to be that:

● closing techniques are strongly related to success
● you should use many types of closes
● you should close frequently during the call.

Starting the research

We started our research into closing in the late 1960s. At the time I was still a university researcher and the only thing I knew about selling was that it was an interaction between people where money changed hands – and, because of that, I reckoned I should be able to find companies who would give me research funds to find out how to make that money change hands more quickly.

I was right. Large multi-national companies *were* interested and I got my funds. But I had the distinct disadvantage that not only had I never sold – I'd never even been out with salespeople to watch them at work. So not knowing where to start, I approached a number of experts for advice. These people, writers, trainers and experienced sales managers, generally suggested that because closing techniques were so crucial to success, that's where I should begin my research. I was particularly impressed by this consensus on closing, because these experts didn't seem to agree about very much else.

Talking with salespeople

My next step was to meet with as many salespeople as possible. And here I became even more impressed. I spent a lot of time just listening to people talking about selling, in branch offices, meetings and informal gatherings. I was surprised how often, and how enthusiastically, the conversation turned to closing techniques. 'I heard a good close the other day . . .', 'Have you tried the gelignite close?', 'You know the old "my pen or yours?" routine, well last week . . .' I was convinced that a good indication of the usefulness of a sales technique would be whether salespeople talked about it in their own time. By that measure, closing was certainly emerging as a winner.

But that's not all: at about that time I was involved in an evaluation study of some training programmes which were being run for experienced sellers. I questioned participants and found something which further convinced me that closing might well be the most important of all selling skills. The average participant could list four different closing techniques, yet was unable to give more than one technique for opening the sale or for handling objections. Less than half of the people I questioned could specify a single tech-nique for investigating customer needs. The group seemed to know more about closing than everything else in selling added together.

Closing for real

Talking to other people certainly influenced my opinions. But there's nothing so powerful as a real-life personal experience – and that's what finally convinced me that closing was by far the most important of all selling skills. I had left my safe university job and had set up an independent research organisation of my own. Now, I realised, selling wasn't just an academic study for me. I had to try to sell my services or go hungry. So I enrolled in a sales training programme – and paid particular attention to the area of closing techniques.

In the week following the programme I had an appointment with a potential client who I'd been talking with for several months in an attempt to sell a research project. I decided to try an alternative close. I'll never forget the result. 'Would you prefer the project to begin in September or in November?' I asked, a little nervously. 'Let's start in September,' my client answered – and I'd got my first big sale. I said the magic words and was rewarded with an order. I doubt if even J. Douglas Edwards, the 'father of closing', could have been more enthusiastic about closing than I was at that moment. For more than a year after my first success, I closed the hell out of everyone. I now realise that I probably cost myself and my company a lot of business during that year. But at the time I was a totally convinced hard closer. After all, my personal experience showed that using an alternative close had given me my first big piece of business. I *knew* closing worked.

113

Initial research

I look back at my enthusiasm for closing with real embarrassment. From what I now know about success in the larger sale, I see closing techniques as both ineffective and dangerous. I've evidence that they lose much more business than they gain. What made me turn against methods that seemed so important to my own success? The rest of this chapter describes the series of studies which finally convinced me that traditional closing techniques have no place in larger sales.

We started our research with the clear expectation that we would find a strong positive link between the number of times a seller closed and whether or not a sale was made. I confidently expected that the magic number of five closes per call, which both Edwards and Schoonmaker recommended, would turn out to be correct.

Our first study took place in a large office equipment company. One way to establish a link between closing and success, we reasoned, would be to travel in the field with sellers and watch how many times they used a closing technique during their call. If the writers on closing were correct we should expect to find that calls with a lot of closes would be more successful than those where the seller didn't close so often. We went out and watched a total of 190 calls. From these we took the 30 where the seller had closed most often and compared their success with the 30 calls where sellers had closed least (Figure 10.1).

As you can see, the results were not what we'd expected. Only 11 of the high close calls resulted in a sale, while 21 of the low close calls did so. This finding wasn't exactly good news for the often quoted 'ideal' figure of five closes per call. But I wasn't discouraged: one small study certainly couldn't shake my faith in closing.

Perhaps, I reasoned, there was something wrong with our methodology. Further examination of our results *did* reveal some potential weaknesses. For example, it's possible – just by chance – that the low close calls were on customers who were prepared to buy anyway, so the seller didn't need to close. Similarly, the high close calls might have been on more resistant customers. Another problem was that our sample, although statistically significant, was small. We had no way to control for intervening variables. Clearly we couldn't, just on the basis of this study, conclude that closing techniques were ineffective. In a letter to my client explaining our findings, I wrote, 'we have not yet succeeded in demonstrating the link between closing and success'. But, looking back we couldn't call this study a resounding victory for the 'close early, close hard and close often' school of selling.

An uneasy feeling . . .

Research isn't only numbers. By watching closing in 190 calls I had begun to get

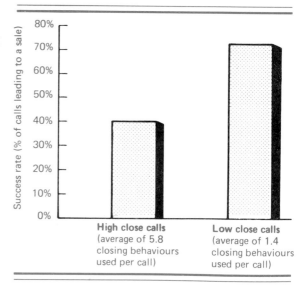

Figure 10.1 Success of high v low close calls

some uneasy feelings which I couldn't quantify. If I'm honest with myself – though I'd not have confessed it at the time – my first misgivings about closing could be traced back to this study. I noticed, for example, a distinct antagonism from some customers, especially professional buyers, when any closing technique was used beyond simply asking for the order. In one of the calls, the seller and I were thrown out by an angry customer after an interchange like this:

Seller: So, Mr Robinson, you see that our product is clearly best for you – if you'll just sign here *(assumptive close)*.

Buyer: Just a moment – I don't see . . . I haven't decided.

Seller: But Mr Robinson, I've shown you how we can improve the efficiency of your office and save you trouble and also money – so if you could decide when you'd like a delivery . . . *(assumptive close)*.

Buyer: I'll do no such thing. I'm not making a decision this week.

Seller: But, as I've explained, this model is in great demand. I can let you have one now, but if you wait till next week, there could be a several month delay. *(standing-room-only close)*.

Buyer: That's a risk I'll have to take.

Seller: Would you prefer a month's trial installation, or would it be better for your budget to buy outright? *(alternative close)*.

Buyer: I'm going to throw you out of my office. Tell me, would you and your friend in the corner prefer to go of your own accord, or would you like me to call security?

As the seller so ruefully remarked to me after the call, it doesn't seem fair when the buyer uses an alternative close to throw you out. We met several episodes like this one and they were enough to sow those first seeds of doubt about closing, particularly in the larger sale.

Attitude problems

At about this time I had the opportunity to look at closing from a completely different angle. The Marketing Director of a major chemical company approached us with a problem. 'I'm worried', he said, 'about some of my salespeople. They've got a wishy-washy attitude to closing sales. They're not aggressive enough. I know that they *can* close – they've had training – it's just that some of them have an attitude problem. Can you help?' It was too good an opportunity to miss. We agreed to devise a closing attitude scale to compare people's attitudes with their sales records. The Marketing Director and I expected to find that those with a favourable attitude to closing should be making more sales. We hoped, ultimately, to devise an attitude test which could be used to screen new applicants. Those who scored high on our closing attitude test should have a greater potential.

In order to find the attitude of the 38 members of the salesforce, we measured their level of agreement (or disagreement) with 15 key statements about closing. The method we used is what's commonly called a *Lickert scale*. If you're the kind of person who likes to test yourself, you'll find that I've included the scale as *Appendix B* to this book, together with instructions for how to score your own attitude to closing. You'll probably get a truer picture of how you feel about closing at present if you score the scale now, before you've had a chance to be influenced by the rest of this chapter.

When we used this test in the chemical company we found that 21 out of the 38 sellers had a score of above 50, which we had taken to be the minimum score for us to classify their attitude as 'favourable'. We then compared sales results to find whether the group with a favourable attitude to closing were, in fact, making more sales. We were taken aback by the results (Figure 10.2).

As you can see, those sellers with a favourable attitude to closing were *below* target, not above it. Our hopes for a closing selection test were dashed. What's worse, my client the Marketing Director didn't believe the results and threatened to fire me unless I could come up with something more convincing.

Explaining the results away

As you might imagine, I tried hard to explain away our findings. It was possible, I argued, that those people whose results were poor were made more anxious by being given the test. As a result they may have cheated and filled in the scale the way they thought management wanted – thus giving those with bad results a falsely positive attitude to closing. But that sounded unconvincing, even to me. I was beginning to have doubts about the effectiveness of closing.

While we were carrying out this study, a number of research teams all over the world were investigating the links between attitude and behaviour. Their results, particularly those of Martin Fishbein, were finding that you couldn't use attitude scales to predict behaviour accurately. Fishbein was showing, for example, that just because you get a high score

on the closing attitude scale, it doesn't mean that in actual sales calls you'll close more often than those with a less favourable attitude. Our own research in other areas was confirming that the links between attitude and behaviour were much weaker than we'd imagined. Consequently we were moving more and more towards methods for directly observing sales behaviour. We were glad to leave attitude and questionnaire studies behind us. The best test of how people actually perform, as we saw in chapter one, is to watch them in action. Our development of new behaviour analysis methods would, we hoped, allow us to do this, and would provide us with much more solid evidence about the effectiveness of closing.

But even though we found some respectable reasons to dismiss our chemical company study, I was still worried. The little data we had gathered was showing some very puzzling things about closing effectiveness. We needed more studies.

The effect of training

An ideal opportunity for further research on closing came when a high-technology company asked us to evaluate some intensive training in closing which they

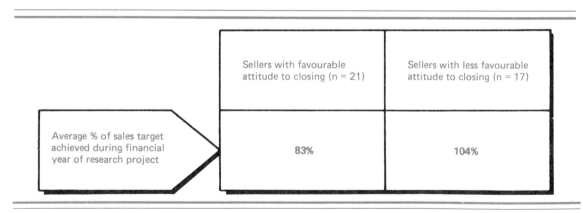

Figure 10.2   Attitude to closing and sales results

were designing. They wanted us to answer two questions:

- Did sellers close more often after the training than before it?
- Was there a relationship between increased closing and sales success?

We were delighted to be presented with another opportunity to test the contribution of closing to sales success. We went out on 86 calls with a group of 47 sellers before the training took place. We wanted to find their existing levels of closing.

After the training we went out with the sellers again, this time to find whether their use of closing had increased and what effect that had on the results of the call. Once again, closing turned out to be negatively related to success. After the training, sellers used more closing techniques – so, in one sense, the training was effective. However, because fewer of the calls succeeded, the overall effect of the training was a *decrease* in sales (see Figure 10.3).

By now we were much less surprised.

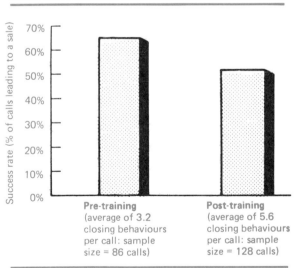

Figure 10.3   Effect of training in closing on success

Finding an association between closing and lost sales was getting to be a habit with us. The trainers we were working with, on the other hand, certainly didn't expect results like these. They were taken aback and advanced several ingenious explanations for the fall in results. One of the possibilities they put forward we were forced to take very seriously. They argued that, by definition, any new skill feels awkward and uncomfortable. Before the training sellers were behaving in their own natural way. After it, they were trying to use new techniques and, inevitably, they were not coming across so naturally to their customers. This, the trainers argued, could cause a temporary drop in sales results. We found this possibility plausible enough to concede that we still didn't have conclusive evidence on the effectiveness of closing. But at least we could test out the idea that the fall in sales resulted from a temporary unnaturalness. What if we went out with the sellers again after six months? By that time the new closing skills would have become part of their natural selling style. We could test whether they were still using the closing techniques and, if so, what impact that was now having on the success of their calls. Everything was arranged for what I hoped would be the first conclusive study of closing effectiveness. Then, a month before the research was due to begin, the company announced a massive reorganisation of its sales force. With all the changes there was no point in going ahead. Another great research study bit the dust and, once again, we found ourselves out in the market looking around for a new company who would give us facilities for studying closing.

A glimmer of light

It was while I was searching for a client to sponsor new studies of closing that I came across a claim by one of the big training companies that their programme in closing increased sales results by more than 30 per cent. In the study we'd just completed, we'd found that closing training caused a *fall* in results. How was it that this company was achieving success? Could it be they were using some closing techniques which were more effective than the ones we'd been investigating? I managed to get hold of their programme and was surprised to find that it didn't contain anything new or different. In fact it was a considerably less sophisticated approach than the one we had been evaluating.

So I made contact with the company and challenged them to show me the evidence which formed the basis of their claim that training in closing could bring a 30 per cent increase in sales. As it happened, their 'research' consisted of letters from satisfied clients, one of whom had said that after the training there had been a 30 per cent increase in results. There was no hard data. But there *was* an important clue. The satisfied clients were all organisations whose size of sale was very small. The 30 per cent claimant, for example, was a company selling magazine subscriptions door-to-door. Then it struck me. All of Huthwaite's studies of closing had been in larger sales. Could it be possible that closing techniques worked when the sale was small, but failed to work as the size of sale increased?

The more I thought about this idea, the more I liked it. There were very good theoretical reasons for believing that this might be true. Closing is a method of putting pressure on the customer. And psychologists now understand quite a lot about the impact of pressure on making decisions. Put very simply, the psychological effect of pressure seems to be this. If I'm asking you to make a very small decision, then – if I pressurise you – it's easier for you to say 'yes' than to have an argument. Consequently, with a small decision, the effect of pressure is positive. But that's not so with large decisions. The bigger the decision, the more negatively

people generally react to pressure.

I make this sound like some great new discovery, but of course it isn't. Since the dawn of history, would-be seducers have known that the effect of pressure is negatively related to the size of decision. The hopeful young man who uses an alternative close such as, 'would you prefer that we sit here, or shall we sit over there?', will usually succeed because he's asking for a small decision. However, the classic alternative close of 'My place or yours?' has a far lower hit rate, because the decision it asks for is much larger.

If my theory was correct, then the larger the decision, the less effective closing techniques were likely to be. But how could we test that out? Was there a way to set up an experiment which could test the effectiveness of closing as the size of the decision grew larger? I didn't want to set up artificial laboratory experiments, yet I didn't know how to validate the idea in any other way. Then one day we were presented with the perfect opportunity on a plate.

The photo shop study

A leading chain of photographic shops had just decided to train their salespeople in closing techniques. It had been a controversial decision for the chain, and not all of their senior management liked the idea. One of their managers had attended a seminar where I'd spoken rather sceptically about closing. He was from the anti-training faction – and he secretly brought us in to test whether the new training was going to be effective.

It's never ideal when clients ask you to do research which is designed to prove that their preconceptions are right. Normally that's the kind of assignment we avoid. But everything else about this research opportunity was so perfect that I just couldn't turn it down. The really attrac-

118

tive element was the shop's policy of rotating their salespeople. One day a seller would work at a counter which sold cheap goods, such as films, tapes and accessories. The next day that same person would move to one of the counters where more expensive goods were sold, such as high-priced cameras, hi-fi and video. We had the perfect way to control for the impact of decision size on closing success. When the store trained its people, we could observe the impact of the training one day when they were selling cheap goods and then, with the same people and the same training, observe them the next day when they were selling goods on the expensive counters. It was ideal.

Closing and decision size

Using the methods taken from our earlier studies, we watched salespeople at work before the training took place. We measured three things:

1 *Transaction time:* how long did each sale or attempted sale take?
2 *Number of closes:* how often did the seller use a closing behaviour during the transaction?
3 *Percentage sale:* what percentage of the transactions resulted in a purchase?

First, let's look at the results collected when people were selling low-value items. Before training in closing, the average transaction time was just over two minutes, the seller used an average of 1.3 closes and 72 per cent of transactions resulted in a sale. What was the effect of the closing training? As you can see, after training the transaction time was cut, the number of closes increased and so did the success rate. As a busy store owner I would be delighted with a result like this. The cut in transaction time means that I can serve more customers or use fewer staff. What's more, although the increase in sales from 72 per cent to 76 per cent isn't big enough to be statistically significant, it *is* in the right direction. Not only is the sale faster, but it also looks to be more successful (see Figure 10.4).

We too were impressed with these results, if only because it was the first time in our research that we'd found anything positive about closing techniques. But the real test was yet to come. Would the training in closing be equally successful with higher value goods?

	Average transaction time	Number of closes per transaction	% transactions resulting in a sale
Before training in closing (83 transactions observed)	2m 11s	1.3	72%
After training in closing (95 transactions observed)	1m 47s	1.9	76%

Figure 10.4   Closing and price: low-value goods

We observed the same salespeople, after the same training. The only difference was that they were now selling more expensive items. We found that the transaction time after training was shorter and the number of closing behaviours predictably increased. But what about success rate? Before training 42 per cent of the interactions we observed had resulted in an order. This was much lower than the success rate with cheaper goods, but that's hardly surprising. People don't usually come in a shop to look at a roll of film and say, 'I'll go away and think about it', although that often happens with more expensive purchases. However, the figure which interested us was the success rate after training. We found that the programme in closing which had increased success with cheap goods had *reduced* success with more expensive goods from 42 per cent down to 33 per cent (see Figure 10.5).

Two conclusions

How should we interpret these results? The first finding is that, with both high- and low-value goods, the average transaction time is reduced as the number of closes is increased. So we can draw the conclusion:

> By forcing the customer into a decision, closing techniques speed the sales transaction.

This would be an important finding – and a big plus for the use of closing techniques – if your business was a low-value retail operation or involved door-to-door selling of low-value products. If there's a queue of customers waiting for your attention, or an infinitely long street with doors on both sides just waiting to be knocked on, then the shorter the sale, the more customers you'll be able to serve.

But that's not usually the problem in larger sales. You normally want *more* time with each customer, not less. In most major account salesforces, the most common complaint is that you can't get *enough* time with the right people. I don't think I've ever heard anyone in larger sales say, 'How can I cut down on the time I'm spending with key decision-makers?'. However, a number of companies have called Huthwaite in to advise them on ways to *increase* sales time with the customers. My point's a simple one: in small sales it's generally desirable to keep transaction time short; in larger sales – for a whole variety of reasons – a shorter

	Average transaction time	Number of closes per transaction	% transactions resulting in a sale
Before training in closing (91 transactions observed)	12m 35s	2.7	42%
After training in closing (91 transactions observed)	8m 40s	4.5	33%

Figure 10.5   Closing and price: high-value goods

transaction time has few advantages and many penalties.

The second conclusion we can draw from our study is about the relationship of closing to price:

> Closing techniques may increase the chances of making a sale with low-priced products. With expensive products or services, they reduce the chances of making a sale.

As we've seen, this conclusion comes not only from our research, but also from the general psychological rule that pressure is more likely to be effective with small decisions than with larger ones. The average price of the high-value goods in our study was just $109. That's peanuts compared with the average decision size in most sales organisations I work with, or for most readers of this book. But if closing techniques become ineffective in a $109 sale, then they are likely to be more ineffective as the size of the decision climbs into the tens or hundreds of thousands. You might argue, of course, that spending $109 of your own money may feel just as big a decision as spending $10 000 from a company budget. And you might be right – nobody really understands the complex psychology of perceived decision size. But the general rule remains. Closing techniques, like all forms of pressure, become less effective as decision size increases.

Closing and client sophistication

It was clear from our studies that closing was less effective as the size of the decision increased. But was that just because of price factors? I wondered whether there might be some other reasons. On the whole, large purchasing decisions are made by more sophisticated customers – such as professional purchas-

ing agents, or senior executives. These people see dozens of sellers each week and may even have been through sales training themselves. Could it be that a closing technique which might work on a less experienced buyer would be ineffective or even have a negative effect on customers who were more sophisticated?

My first indication that this might be true came when I was working with the central purchasing department of British Petroleum. I'd been observing their buyers at work, doing research from the other side of the table. One of the BP senior buyers was particularly ill-disposed towards the use of closing techniques. 'It's not closing itself that I object to,' he told me, 'it's the arrogant assumption that I'm stupid enough to be manipulated into buying through the use of tricks. Whenever a standard closing technique is used on me it reduces the respect between us – it destroys the professional business relationship. But I've got my own way of dealing with it, as you'll see.'

The following day I was watching an attempted sale and saw the buyer's method in action. The seller was in the vending machine business and supplied plastic cups. At one point in the call he used an assumptive close, saying, 'Mr P., you've agreed that our cups are cheaper than your present supplier, so shall we make our first delivery of, say, 20 000 cups next month?'. The buyer said nothing. He opened a drawer in his desk and slowly took out a box of 5 x 3 index cards. He shuffled through the box and selected one with *assumptive close* typed on it, placing it face up on his desk. 'That's your first chance,' he said, 'I give people two. If you use just one more closing technique on me, then it's no sale. Just so you know what I'm watching for, look through these cards.' And he handed the cards across his desk to the seller. On each card a well-known closing technique was typed. The seller went pale – but didn't try closing again.

Working with buyers

Was this buyer an exception? Some monster with a perverted hatred of closing? I don't think so. Most professional buyers have an unfavourable view of closing techniques. I once trained professional buyers from three large organisations in a programme which developed negotiating skills. I circulated a questionnaire among 54 of these buyers which included the question:

> 'If you detect that a seller is using closing techniques while selling to you, what effect, if any, does that have on your likelihood of buying?'

Their answers were

more likely to buy	2
indifferent	18
less likely to buy	34

Nobody knows better than I do that this type of questionnaire data isn't a very reliable guide to actual behaviour. But, despite all the limitations of this kind of evidence, closing techniques certainly don't seem to be favourites with professional buyers. I've seen a number of books and training programmes which claim that sophisticated buyers react very positively to the use of closing techniques because it's a sign they are dealing with a professional. That's dangerous nonsense. There's not one scrap of evidence to back that sort of assertion. The few research studies which exist all suggest that more sophisticated buyers react negatively to the use of closing.

Closing and post-sale satisfaction

In chapter two I pointed out that one of the characteristic differences between small and large sales was that larger sales usually involved some form of ongoing relationship with the customer. Your job doesn't just end with the order. So it's an important question to ask what effect closing has on the post-sale relationship. Unfortunately we've never had an opportunity to study this in larger sales. However, we did help one retail organisation carry out a consumer goods study which has some disturbing implications for sales of *any* size.

The training manager of a retail chain had attended a seminar run by Huthwaite on behaviour measurement, and he was keen to try his hand at some research. He asked me for help in choosing a suitable project. 'How about a study on closing?' I suggested. Some of the sales people in his organisation had been trained in closing techniques, so he decided to investigate whether customer satisfaction after the purchase was related to the seller's training in closing.

Between three and five days after the purchase, he and his team followed up 145 customers and asked them to rate, on a 10-point scale:

- their satisfaction with the goods they had purchased
- the probability, if they were to make similar purchases in the future, that they would buy from the same shop.

The results are shown in Figure 10.6.

As you can see, the sellers who had been trained in closing had lower satisfaction ratings on both questions. What does this mean? The most likely interpretation is that, in using closing techniques, sellers put pressure on customers to make a decision. Most people are less satisfied with decisions where they feel they've been pressurised than they are with those decisions they believe they've made entirely of their own free will. This suggests there's even more reason to be cautious about the use of closing techniques in larger sales, where the customer's post-sale satisfaction may be an important factor in future selling success.

I could of course, criticise some elements of this study. It doesn't for example, have any behavioural data collected during the actual sales themselves. And there's another possible weakness – the shop had trained more of their younger people than of their most experienced sellers. So perhaps this study is saying that customers are less satisfied with purchases from more junior salespeople. But, despite any criticisms of its methodology, this study is one of the very few which has ever tried to collect data on the relationship between sales training and post-sale satisfaction. Until more detailed studies come along, I advise you to heed its warning.

Why is the rest of the army out of step?

For several years after I'd collected all this data about the effectiveness of closing, I was very reluctant to share it with other people. As I showed early in the chapter,

closing was not only seen by the majority of writers as the most important part of the sale, it was almost a religion with many salespeople. On the few occasions I'd mentioned these findings in public, I'd had a bad reception. As I mentioned earlier, I was once pulled off the stage by an angry sales trainer in Los Angeles who didn't like the research I'd presented there. History is full of stories about researchers whose ideas aren't recognised at first. It wasn't the rejection that worried me. My concern was that it didn't seem possible that I was right and so many others were wrong. Experienced salespeople, their managers, their trainers and the experts who write books on how to sell aren't fools. How is it they could devote so much time and energy to a set of techniques which not only don't work but, in larger sales, are actively counter-productive? What's so compelling about closing?

What makes a compulsive closer?

The answer came to me during a seminar

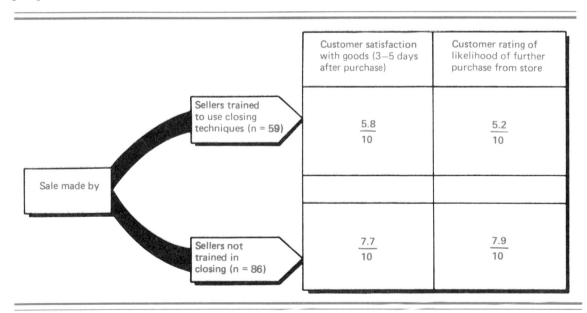

Figure 10.6   Closing and customer satisfaction

	Customer satisfaction with goods (3–5 days after purchase)	Customer rating of likelihood of further purchase from store
Sellers trained to use closing techniques (n = 59)	$\frac{5.8}{10}$	$\frac{5.2}{10}$
Sellers not trained in closing (n = 86)	$\frac{7.7}{10}$	$\frac{7.9}{10}$

I was running with Roger Harrison. Roger was conducting the session and the topic was ineffective behaviour patterns and their causes. He was explaining that sometimes people will continue to do things which don't bring results, but they will nevertheless believe strongly that what they are doing is effective. 'Hmm, like salespeople who believe in closing', I thought. Roger went on to suggest that there are only two reasons why anyone would continue to behave in a way which is unsuccessful. Either they are crazy, or else *there's something in their environment which is rewarding and encouraging the use of the ineffective behaviour.*

The more I thought about this, the more it gave me the explanation I had been looking for. I remembered the time when I had been so enthusiastic about closing. How did I get hooked into becoming a hard closer? It all went back to the time I nervously tried my first alternative close, 'Would you prefer the project to begin in September, or in November?' In replying, 'let's start in September', my client *rewarded* my use of a close by giving me the business. I said the words – I got the order.

When I stopped to think about it, closing behaviours were the only ones, out of the 116 we studied in our research, which were directly rewarded or reinforced by orders. Like so many other salespeople, because my close was rewarded with an order, I'd somehow assumed that using the close had *caused* the order. Of course, from what I now know, it was the way I'd developed my client's needs which brought me the business. It was nothing to do with my close – the project would have gone ahead with or without my new closing technique.

At last I understood why closing received so much attention in selling. It was the most immediately rewarded of all sales behaviours. Ask the customers a good question which develops needs and you don't instantly get rewarded with an order. But use some magic closing catch-phrase at the moment of decision and – some of the time – you'll get a rewarding 'Yes, I'll buy'. (Incidentally, any reader who understands the theory of reinforcement will also recognise that 'some-of-the-time' rewards are even more powerful than 'all-of-the-time' rewards in causing a behaviour to continue.)

As a result of this insight, I became more comfortable about our research and its implications. It was indeed possible that our research was right and most of the rest of the world was out of step. Since our studies, of course, many other people have come to the same conclusion that closing techniques are ineffective or even damaging in larger sales. I'm delighted nowadays, when I talk to people about closing to find that I no longer get the antagonism that our work once aroused. I've been seen by many people as a sworn enemy of all closing techniques. If J. Douglas Edwards is the father of closing, I've sometimes been described as its assassin. But that's not quite fair. In low-value sales, with unsophisticated customers and where you don't have continuing customer relationship, then closing techniques can work very effectively – and I've no criticism of their use. But I'm assuming that, as a reader of this book, your business comes from the larger sale, you deal with professional buyers and you form lasting relationships with your customers. If so, then closing techniques will make you *less* effective and will reduce your chances of getting the business.

But you must close

It sounds as though I'm saying that you shouldn't try to close the sale – that because closing techniques are ineffective, you should somehow wait for the sale to close itself. Clearly that doesn't work either. Many sales managers have groaned inwardly as they've listened to their less experienced people reach the stage of the call which we term *obtaining commitment*, and they've heard something like:

New seller: So, is there anything else I can tell you about this product?

Customer: No thanks. I think you've answered all my questions.

New seller: Good. Good. You're sure there's nothing else I haven't covered?

Customer: Not that I can think of.

New seller: Okay *(horrid pause)* uh . . . perhaps I didn't mention that it's got dual voltage.

Customer: Yes. Well I'm overdue for another meeting and . . .

New seller: *(With some depression)* it's also got an instruction manual in Spanish . . . if you need Spanish.

Customer: Look Mr Newman, I've got to go.

New seller: Um. Are you *sure* I've answered all your questions?

What's wrong here? An inexperienced salesperson is afraid to bring the call to a conclusion and, as a result, the customer is getting impatient.

This certainly happens in real life – and it's often noticeable in the selling of professional services. We've worked with First National Bank of Chicago, using Huthwaite's models to train calling officers. David Zehren of First Chicago, while agreeing with us that closing techniques are generally over-used in major industrial sales, points out that in banking there's often the opposite problem. 'We haven't had a problem with excessive use of closing techniques', he explains. 'If anything, we feel it necessary to lean in the other direction. Customers expect it. They get irritated by calls that don't have a clear understanding of what comes next.'

David Zehren isn't the only one to voice this concern. We've worked with several of the big eight accounting firms, and their training staff share the same perception. If over-use of closing is a problem in many industrial and capital goods sales, then it's total absence may be an equally severe problem in some service industries. While most of our clients fully accept that the most crucial part of the sales call is developing needs, those in the professional services area justifiably want their people to take a stronger role in obtaining commitment from customers.

Sales training, over the years, has clearly put much too great an emphasis on closing. But it would be equally unfortunate if we let the pendulum swing so far the other way that we began to teach people never to close at all.

There's hard data which emphasises that absence of closing can be a real danger. We carried out some research with Bob Boyles of American Airlines to find whether inability to use *any* closing was even less effective than closing too often. Boyles and his team had been experimenting with some of our behaviour analysis techniques in American Airlines to monitor the skills of their sales agents.

The success rate in calls with no closing whatever was only 22 per cent, compared with a 61 per cent success rate in one-close calls. Notice, however, that the least successful calls were those with more than two closing behaviours, where the success rate was below 20 per cent. So it seems that, despite all the disavantages of closing techniques, calls with no closing whatsoever are unlikely to be effective (Figure 10.7).

Where do we go from here?

The American Airlines investigation involved relatively small sales. Although

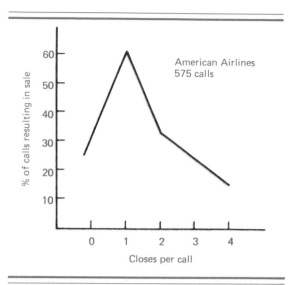

Figure 10.7   Number of closes v success rate

I'm not sure whether we'd have found the same results in a comparable study of major sales, this research does raise an important issue. The seller *must* obtain some kind of commitment from the customer for the call to be a success. But how can you get a commitment from your customer without the penalties which come from using closing techniques?

Everything I've written so far in this chapter is about how *not* to obtain commitment. I've said that traditional closing techniques are ineffective or have a negative effect when:

● the sale is large, involving high value goods
● the customer is sophisticated, for example, a professional buyer
● there is a continuing post-sale relationship with the customer.

All that I've said suggests that closing techniques are not the best way to obtain commitment from the customer in a major sale. But what *should* you do? As we've seen, doing nothing isn't effective either. The sale doesn't close itself.

Obtaining commitment: four successful actions

Huthwaite's studies of success in the major sale show that effective salespeople use rather simple and straightforward ways of obtaining commitment. We found that there were four clear actions which successful people tended to use, which helped them obtain commitment from their customers.

1   Paying attention to investigating and demonstrating capability

Successful salespeople devote their main efforts to the investigating and demonstrating capability stages. In particular, they take much more time over the investigating part of the call. Less-successful sellers rush through the investigating stage. As a result, they don't do such an effective job of uncovering, understanding and developing the needs of their customers. You won't obtain commitment, in a larger sale, unless the customer clearly perceives a need for what you offer. The most effective people we observed were the ones who did an outstanding job of building needs during the investigating stage. As a result of the questions they asked, their customers came to realise that they had an urgent need to buy. You don't require closing techniques with a customer who wants to buy. So the first successful strategy for obtaining customer commitment is to concentrate your attention on the investigating stage of the call (see Figure 10.8). If you can convince buyers that they need what you are offering, then they will often close the sale for you.

2 Checking that key concerns are covered

In larger sales, both the product and the customer needs are likely to be relatively complex. As a result, there may well be

126

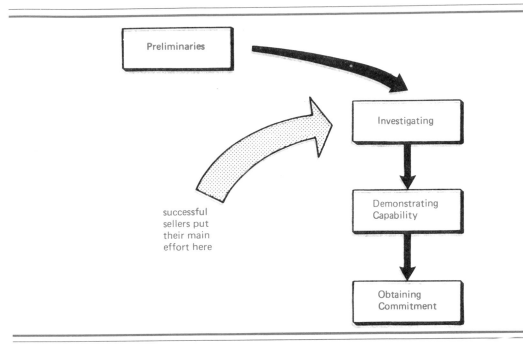

Figure 10.8 Four stages of a sales call

areas of confusion or doubt in the customer's mind as the point of commitment nears. Less-successful sellers go ahead and close, ignoring the possibility that their customers may still have unanswered questions. That's often how they've been taught to sell. Most sales training programmes actually recommend that you use closing as a means of bringing doubts or unanswered questions to the surface. But that's not what successful salespeople do. We found that sellers who were most effective in obtaining commitment from their customers would invariably take the initiative and ask the buyer whether there were any further points or concerns which needed to be addressed.

From our observations, a doubt or concern which is given in response to a closing technique tends to be antagonistic, as this brief example illustrates:

Seller: *(using assumptive close)* . . . so I'll arrange for our technical people to set up a demonstration next week.

Buyer: *(Who has an unresolved concern)* Hey, wait a minute, I'm not sure whether I'm ready for a demonstration.

Seller: *(Using alternative close)* Then would it be better if, instead of setting it up for next week, I set it up for the week after?

Buyer: *(Feeling pressured)* Now, not so fast. You still haven't explained how this leasing arrangement would work. What are you trying to hide?

By using closing techniques it's true that the seller has brought the customer's concern to the surface. But was it necessary to do so in such an antagonistic way? A more successful seller would have checked that all key concerns were covered before trying to bring the call to a conclusion. For example:

Seller: *(Checking all key concerns are covered)* Well, I think that covers everything Ms Brown. But before we go further, could I check whether there are any areas which you feel I should tell you more about?

Buyer: Yes, you haven't mentioned the terms of the leasing arrangement.

Seller: Then let me cover that now. The way it works is . . .

In this example, the customer's concern has been brought to the surface by the seller's initiative. Instead of being an antagonistic protest from the buyer, it has become a simple query.

3 Summarising the benefits

In a larger sale the call may have taken several hours and covered a wide range of topics. It's unlikely that the customer has a clear picture of everything which has been discussed. Successful salespeople pull the threads together by summarising key points of the discussion before moving to the commitment. In smaller sales, the use of a summary may not be necessary, but in a larger sale it will almost always be a helpful way to bring key points into focus just before the decision. So, summarise key points – especially benefits.

4 Proposing a commitment

Many books on selling point out that the simplest of all closing methods is to just ask for the order. Consequently the term, 'asking for the order' is a common one in sales training. But, from our studies, 'asking' is *not* what successful sellers do. In all the other stages of the sale, asking behaviours are much more successful than giving behaviours – as we'll see in later chapters. But it's here, at the point of commitment, that successful sellers don't ask – they tell. The most natural, and most effective, way to bring a call to a successful conclusion is to suggest an appropriate next step to the customer. For example:

Seller: (*Checking key concerns*) Is there anything else which we need to cover?

Buyer: No, I think we've discussed everything.

Seller: (*Summarising the benefits*) Yes, we've certainly seen how the new system will speed your order processing and how it will be simpler to use than your present one. We've also discussed the way in which it can help you control costs. In fact, there seem to be some impressive benefits from changing, particularly as a new system would get rid of those reliability problems which have been worrying you.

Buyer: Yes, when you add it all up, there's a lot of value to us from making the change.

Seller: (*Proposing a commitment*) Then could I suggest that the most logical next step would be for you and your accountant to come and see one of these systems in operation.

I've said that proposing a commitment is a simple, natural way to bring a call to a successful conclusion. But I'm oversimplifying a little. Before you can propose a commitment you've got to know what the most appropriate commitment would be. Unlike the smaller sale, where the only commitment is an order, in the larger sale there may be a *range* of possible commitments you could suggest. You might, for example, want to:

● meet the buyer's boss
● agree to a test run of your product
● set up a demonstration
● undertake a survey
● obtain access to another part of the organisation.

How do you know which commitment to propose? Put simply, there are two characteristics of the commitments proposed by successful salespeople.

1 They *advance* the sale. As a result of the commitment, the sale will move forward in some way.
2 The commitment proposed is the

highest *realistic* commitment that the customer is able to give. Successful sellers never push the customer beyond achievable limits.

Techniques to help your selling

I've suggested, in this chapter, that classic closing techniques don't work:

- in the larger sale
- with sophisticated buyers
- where your objective is to maintain an ongoing relationship with your customer.

So I strongly advise you to avoid them. Instead, I've outlined a simple alternative approach:

1 Successful closing of the call starts with a realistic call objective. Before you make *any* call, ask yourself what you are trying to achieve. In particular, ask how you will obtain an advance (the active move forward described in chapter three). Don't be content with continuation objectives like 'collecting information' or 'keeping the door open'. But, equally, don't set unrealistically high goals. The important thing is to keep the sale moving forward. You should 'close' for an action which progresses the sale.

2 Give your main attention to SPIN® questions for developing needs in the investigating stage of the call. In that way, you have a customer who wants to buy, which makes it very much easier to obtain commitment. I find that a useful test of how much commitment

I can obtain is the amount of *value* I've built up during the call. If the customer doesn't feel that a problem is worth solving, the best closing in the world won't help. So, if my call objective is for a large commitment – for example, an advance where I want the customer's agreement to give me access to a senior decision-maker – then I know I must use implication and need-payoff questions to build value or I'll get turned down. In contrast, suppose all I want is access to a junior technical person, then I can usually obtain that commitment with or without the use of SPIN® questions.

3 When you are obtaining a commitment from your customers, use the three steps which we found in successful calls:

- *check you've covered key concerns*
- *summarise the benefits*
- *propose a realistic commitment.*

Above all, keep it simple. Tricky closing techniques have no place in the larger sale. If you've done a really good job of building needs, then these three simple steps are the most effective.

I've saved the last word on closing the sale for an old friend and colleague of mine, the Swedish consultant Hans Stennek. At a time when my research was controversial and was generally rejected by most people in selling, Hans was very supportive. 'I've never been a believer in closing,' he told me, 'because my objective is not to close the sale but to open a relationship.' I couldn't have said it better myself.

11

Turning theory into practice

One of my favourite words, 'entelechy', is so little known that listeners reach for a dictionary whenever I use it. That's a pity, because the word fills a serious gap in the English language and it deserves to be in everyday circulation. It means the becoming actual of what was potential – turning something into practical usefulness as opposed to theoretical elegance. Entelechy is the subject of this chapter. turning the potential of our research into something which will be practically useful to you in your selling.

and for our clients. Your challenge is a more demanding one. Improving your skills is hard work; there's no instant formula for better selling. Success in any skill – whether we're talking about golf, playing the piano or selling – rests on concentrated, tedious and frustrating practice. It's quite realistic for you to expect a significant increase in your sales results if you follow the advice in this book and *really practise* the skills. But that's the hard bit. For each reader who adequately practises, there's likely to be a dozen who fall by the wayside.

Skills are hard to learn

There's no easy way to convert theoretical models into practical skills. You've read this book, but that doesn't mean the knowledge you've gained will automatically translate itself into improved selling ability. Reading a book on selling doesn't, of itself, improve your selling skills, any more than reading a book about swimming will teach you how to swim. The challenge for both author and reader in any book with pretensions to being practical is *entelechy* – turning theory into practical action.

To help meet my part of the challenge, I'll draw on Huthwaite's worldwide experience of training many thousands of people to improve their selling skills. I'll share some of the principles and practices which have worked successfully for us

How to learn a skill

Why do people find it so difficult to learn skills? It's not just because of the hard work – we're accustomed to putting work into learning new knowledge. You've demonstrated that already, through the time and energy you've invested in reading this book – in acquiring *knowledge* about how to sell. Yet I wonder how many readers will invest an equivalent amount of effort to turn their knowledge into practice. The sad fact is that we generally work harder and more effectively to learn knowledge than to translate our knowledge into skills. Perhaps entelechy is such a rare word because it refers to something we so rarely do.

It's my personal belief that the main reason why people have such trouble improving their skills is that they've never thought about the basic techniques of skill learning. At school our success depends on developing techniques for learning knowledge – and most of us get quite good at it. But what did school do to systematically help us learn skills? With the exception of sports, the answer for most people is little or nothing. So, before I talk about what skills you should practise, it might be useful for me to take a small diversion and begin with *how*. How can you learn *any* skill efficiently and with minimum pain?

The four golden rules for learning skills

Over the years I've found that most people can greatly improve their skills-learning if they stick by four simple rules.

Rule 1   practise only one behaviour at a time

Most people, when they work on improving their skills, try to do too much at once. I can imagine people reading this book and saying, 'I'm going to cut out closing techniques and, in future, I'll ask more problem questions. Then, instead of jumping in with solutions – which is what I usually do – I'll hold back and ask implication questions . . . oh, and need-payoff questions too, of course. And I'll also work on avoiding features and advantages. Instead I'll offer more benefits and . . .' *Stop!* If that's how you're thinking then, in terms of learning, you're dead. People who successfully learn complex skills do so by practising one behaviour at a time – not by half practising two, and certainly not by trying to handle ten at once.

Last year I was on a flight to Australia and I found myself sitting opposite a delightful man called Tom Landry. As an Englishman, my sports are cricket and croquet – I knew nothing of American foot-

ball. Consequently it wasn't until well into the conversation that it emerged that Mr Landry was a famous football coach. I confess, right up to that moment, I'd mistakenly thought the Dallas Cowboys were a travelling rodeo show. So I was fascinated when Tom Landry explained a little about the sophisticated and complex task which is involved in coaching a major football team.

'Your job is teaching people skills', I prompted him. 'If you had to put forward just one principle for successfully learning a skill, what would it be?' He didn't hesitate. 'Work on one thing at a time,' he replied, 'and get it right.' Benjamin Franklin said much the same in 1771. In his *Autobiography*, he gives a masterly account of how to break a complex skill into its component behaviours and then how to work on improving it one behaviour at a time. With authorities like Franklin and Landry to support me, I don't hesitate to put forward the first, and most important, principle for getting value from this book:

Start by picking *just one* behaviour to practise. Don't move on to the next until you're confident you've got the first behaviour right.

Rule 2   try the new behaviour at least three times

The first time you try anything new it's bound to feel uncomfortable. It's not only new shoes which hurt at first. Suppose, for example, you decide to practise implication questions. You're keeping Rule 1 in mind, so you're going to concentrate only on implication questions, not on the other behaviours we've covered. Off you go into a call. Do the new implication questions roll off your tongue in a smooth convincing sequence? Not on your life! When you ask them you sound self-conscious, artificial and awkward. And, because of that, you don't make a particularly positive impression on the customer.

After the call, if you're like most people we've trained, you'll be tempted to conclude that implication questions didn't help you sell – so you'd better drop them and try something different next call.

If you draw that conclusion, of course, you're making a big mistake. You have to try any new behaviour several times before it becomes practised enough to be both comfortable and effective. The new skill needs to be 'broken in'. It's not just in selling that this happens. Whenever you try to improve *any* skill, at first it feels awkward and it doesn't go right. I once asked a sample of 200 people who had each taken golf lessons from a professional, whether their next round was better or worse. Out of the 200, 157 said that they scored *worse* after the lesson than before it.

What's the remedy? The principle which I use personally – and which I recommend to those I train – is this:

> Never judge whether a new behaviour is effective until you've tried it *at least three times*.

Rule 3   quantity before quality

Remember the old-fashioned way to learn a foreign language? You try to say a few words. 'No', says your teacher, 'that's the incorrect tense – you should be using a pluperfect.' You try again. 'Wrong', the teacher warns you, 'you've got the tense right, but this is an irregular verb.' With some nervousness you make a third attempt. 'No,' your teacher tells you, 'this time the tense is right, the verb is right but your pronunciation is terrible.' Notice that every one of the teacher's comments is about the *quality* of your skill. Many of us struggled for years to learn a language this way. At the end of it we were able to hesitantly but correctly pronounce a few sentences with the right verbs, tenses and word orders. Most of us never reached the point, despite several years of emph-

asis on quality, where we could speak the language confidently and comfortably.

In contrast, let's look at modern language training. Students are told, 'Never mind about pronunciation, don't worry about tenses. For now, word order doesn't matter and we don't care if you forget the difference between regular and irregular verbs. The only thing we want you to do is speak it, speak it and speak it'. The emphasis, in other words, is on quantity rather than quality – talking a *lot* is more important than talking *well*. Many convincing experiments have shown that this approach, which puts emphasis on the *quantity* of speech, can greatly speed the learning of language skills. At the end of a single year, students are talking the new language more confidently than those who have spent five times as long learning in the old quality-first manner. What's more surprising, is that by talking the language a lot, quality has improved too. In fact the correctness of language, measured by pronunciation and grammar test, is higher in those taught by the quantity approach than those taught by older quality methods. So, in language training at least, speaking it a lot wins hands down over speaking it well.

But does the same principle apply to a skill like selling? Yes – without question it does. Our studies have consistently shown that the fastest way to learn a new sales behaviour is through using a quantity method. Let me give you an example of what I mean. There was a well-known multinational company whose name, for reasons of protecting the guilty, had better remain anonymous. This company liked the SPIN® model and wanted to produce a sales training programme based on it. Their designers spent nine months producing a $650 000 extravaganza which was meant to be the ultimate in sales training. *Quality* was their motto. So, for example, in their programme you couldn't just ask problem questions. Oh no, that wouldn't do at all because you might not be asking the right *quality* of questions. Instead they built a four-stage model of how to ask a problem question, with special attention to three ways in which problem questions could be smoothly linked to situation questions and sundry other techniques to ensure that any problem question – when the poor student ultimately got round to asking it – would have the right quality. The result of their efforts was a 74-step model which was so demotivating and cumbersome that it didn't even get through its pilot without a walkout by confused and angry learners. Tracking students in the field afterwards, we found that they were asking an average of 1.6 problem questions per call – no different from the pre-training level.

Huthwaite – maybe because we'd played no part in this monstrous design – was selected to be the bearer of ill tidings to corporate headquarters. I had to tell the decision-maker that he'd just spent most of his training budget on a programme which was so bad that it couldn't even stagger through its pilot test. When his initial rage had subsided to a gentle gibber, he was able to ask, 'What shall I do?'. We suggested that for considerably less than one tenth of the cost, a programme could be designed which would be much more effective. 'Concentrate on *quantity*', we advised him, 'and you'll get the results you're looking for.' Sure enough, just two months later, we had a programme based on methods closely resembling effective language training. We didn't care whether questions were asked well or poorly but we *did* care that people asked a lot of them. At the end of the training, in the final role plays, students were asking a dozen problem questions. Back out in the field, real-life responses from customers soon told them which of these questions worked best and – as in language training – quality improved dramatically. The $650 000 quality-based programme was scrapped and our cheap but effective quantity-based programme was adopted in its place across the company's three largest divisions.

134

Exactly the same principle applies to your own selling when you're trying to learn a new behaviour:

When you're practising, concentrate on quantity: use a *lot* of the new behaviour. Don't worry about quality issues, such as whether you're using it smoothly, or whether there might be a better way to phrase it. Those things get in the way of effective skills learning. Use the new behaviour often enough and quality will look after itself.

Rule 4   practise in safe situations

I once ran a negotiating skills programme for company chairmen. On the last day, one of the participants asked me an innocent sounding question. 'Tomorrow', he explained, 'I'll be going into the biggest negotiation of my career – I'm selling my company. What lessons from this programme should I concentrate on during the negotiation?' I think my answer shocked him. 'Forget every single thing you've heard on this programme', I advised him, 'otherwise you'll spend the rest of your life regretting you came here'.

Let me give you some similar advice. If you've just finished this book and you're about to visit your most important account, then forget everything I've written. It's a strange quirk of human nature that we usually try to practise new skills in key situations which are important enough to justify the effort of trying something new. That's a terrible mistake. As we've seen, new skills are uncomfortable and awkward. They may even have a negative effect on the customer. If you try them out in crucial situations, then you're likely to be unsuccessful. Suppose you've decided to ask more need-payoff questions. Don't practise on your biggest account. Instead, begin with small accounts, or customers you know well, or in areas where you've nothing to lose if you fail. In other words:

Always try out new behaviours in safe

situations until they feel comfortable. Don't use important sales to practise new skills.

These rules combine to provide a simple strategy for learning or improving your skills. Although my purpose here is to focus on improving selling skills, these four basic rules will help you improve *any* skills, from making love to flying aeroplanes (Figure 11.1).

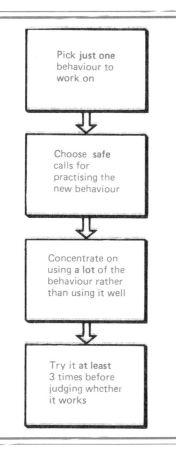

Figure 11.1 Strategies for learning a new skill

A summary

Let's summarise the key points we've made in earlier chapters.

Four stages of a sales call (Chapter 3)

Almost every sales call progresses through four distinct stages:

- *Preliminaries:* the 'warming up' events at the start of the call
- *Investigating:* finding out facts, information and needs
- *Demonstrating capability:* showing that you've got something worthwhile to offer.
- *Obtaining commitment:* gaining an agreement to proceed to a further stage of the sale.

Preliminaries (Chapter 9)

We've suggested that there's no single best way to open a sales call. Successful people are flexible and rarely open two calls in the same way. Two opening techniques recommended by sales training programmes – relating to the buyer's personal interests and the 'opening benefit statement' – have unintended drawbacks and should be used with caution.

Investigating (Chapters 3-6)

Our research showed that the traditional distinction between open and closed questions didn't predict success in larger sales. Instead we discovered the SPIN® sequence of questions (Situation, Problem, Implication, Need-payoff) which successful people use to uncover and develop customer needs in the larger sale.

Demonstrating capability (Chapter 7)

The traditional definition of a benefit – a statement which shows how your product can be used or can help the customer

– works in small sales but fails as the sale grows larger. In major sales, the most effective type of benefit shows how your product or service meets an *explicit need* which has been expressed by the customer.

Obtaining commitment (Chapter 10)

Closing techniques are effective in smaller sales but they don't work in larger ones. Our studies showed that the simplest way to obtain commitment was also the most effective:

- *check* you've covered key concerns
- *summarise* the benefits
- *propose* an appropriate level of commitment.

The sequence of call stages are outlined in Figure 11.2.

The SPIN® Model (Chapters 5 & 6)

The SPIN® model for uncovering and developing needs consists of four types of questions:

- *Situation questions:* about facts, background and what the customer is doing now. Asking too many situation questions can bore or irritate the customer. Research shows that successful people ask them sparingly – so that each question has a purpose.
- *Problem questions:* about the customer's problems, difficulties or dissatisfactions. Problem questions are strongly

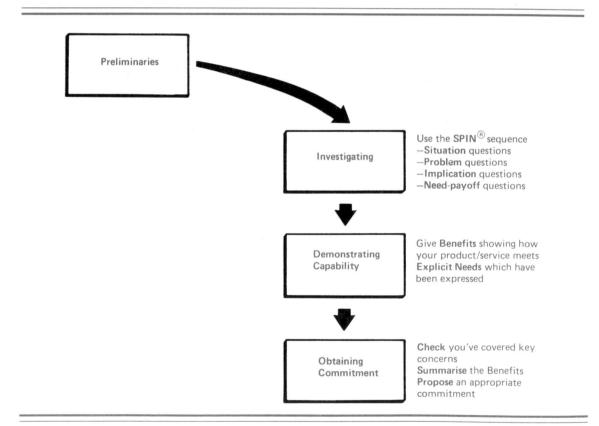

Figure 11.2   Call stages

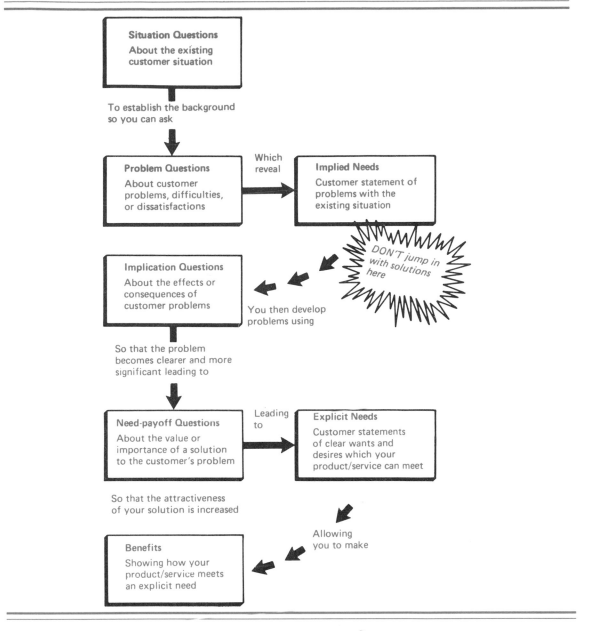

Figure 11.3 The SPIN® model

linked to success in smaller sales, but are less powerful in major sales.

- *Implication questions:* about the consequences or effects of a customer's problems. Successful calls usually contain a high level of implication questions. The ability to develop implications is a crucial skill in the larger sale because it increases the custo-

mer's perception of *value* in the solution you offer.

- *Need-payoff questions:* about the value, usefulness or utility which the customer perceives in a solution. As with implication questions, need-payoff questions are strongly linked to success in the major sale.

137

The SPIN® model is often used sequentially, starting with situation questions to establish the background, then problem questions to uncover difficulties, then implication questions to develop the seriousness of a problem and, finally, need-payoff questions to get the customer telling *you* the benefits from your solution. However, as I've said before, the SPIN® sequence isn't a rigid formula. To be effective it must be used flexibly. The SPIN® model is shown in Figure 11.3.

A strategy for learning the SPIN® behaviours

My colleagues at Huthwaite have worked with many thousands of salespeople, helping them use the models I've described in this book. We've experimented with dozens of different training approaches. In large corporations we've generally adopted designs which make very sophisticated use of advanced learning techniques. At the other extreme, we've also tried to develop some very simple ways to help individual salespeople improve their skills. Alas, there's no free lunch in the training business. It's an unfortunate truth that our more elaborate and sophisticated training designs have generally brought much better productivity gains than the simpler ones. That's made us a little self-conscious about recommending simple steps for improving your skills.

Even so, there *are* some fairly easy, commonsense ways to take the research findings in this book and turn them into useful practice. We've found that there are four pieces of implementation advice which people invariably find helpful.

1 Focus on the investigating stage

Many people, when they plan calls, think about what they will tell the customer, not what they will ask. They concentrate, in other words, on the demonstrating capabilities stage of the call. That's a mistake. However well you demonstrate capability, you'll have little impact unless you've first developed needs, so that the customer *wants* the capability you're offering. The same is true of the obtaining commitment stage. Unless the customer wants what you have to offer, you're going to find it difficult to get a commitment. Focus your efforts on the investigating stage. Practise your questioning skills and the other stages of the call generally look after themselves. If you know how to develop needs – to get your customers to *want* the capabilities you offer – then you'll have no problem showing benefits or obtaining commitment. The key selling skill is in the investigating stage, using the SPIN® questions to get your customers to genuinely feel a need for your product.

2 Develop questions in the SPIN® sequence

Don't rush in to practise the high-powered implication and need-payoff questions until you feel you've a solid and comfortable grasp of the simpler situation and problem questions.

- First decide whether you're asking enough questions of *any* type. If you've built up selling patterns which involve telling – in other words, if you're giving a lot of features and advantages – start by just asking more questions. Most of the questions you ask will be *situation questions*, but that's fine. Just keep asking questions for a few weeks until asking feels as comfortable as telling.
- Next, plan and ask *problem questions*. Aim, in the average call, to ask a customer about problems, difficulties and dissatisfactions at least half a dozen times. Concentrate on building up the *quantity* of your problem ques-

138

tions, don't worry about whether or not each question is a good one.

- If you feel you're doing an effective job of uncovering customer problems, it's time to move on to *implication questions*. These are more difficult to ask and you may need a couple of months' practice before you become entirely comfortable with implication questions. Plan them carefully. A good starting point would be to re-read the example transcript in chapter six. Then, in place of the problem in the transcript, put a problem of your own, which one of your products could solve for your customer. Using the questions in the transcript as a model, try to write some examples of implication questions you could ask which would make your customer feel the problem is serious enough to justify action. When I'm planning implication questions, I find it's useful to imagine a customer who's saying, 'So what? Yes, I've got that problem – but I don't think it's serious'. I list the arguments I'd use to convince the customer that the problem really *is* serious – it's causing a loss of efficiency, it's increasing her costs, it's de-motivating her better people. Then I turn each of my arguments into a question – 'what effect is the problem having on your efficiency?', 'How much is it increasing your costs?', or 'What impact does that have on the motivation of your better people?'

- Finally, when you're comfortable with situation, problem and implication questions, turn your attention to *need-payoff questions*. Instead of giving benefits to the customer, concentrate on asking questions which get the customer to tell *you* the benefits. Ask questions like, 'How would that help you?', 'What do *you* see as the pluses of this approach?', or 'Is there any other way our product could be useful?'. Again, don't worry about whether you're asking need-payoff questions *well*. Concentrate on quantity – on asking *lots* of them.

3 Analyse your product in problem solving terms

Stop thinking about your products in terms of their features and advantages. Instead, think of each product in terms of its problem-solving capability. Analyse products by listing the problems they are designed to solve. Then use your list to plan questions you can use in calls. By thinking of your products this way, you'll find it easier to adopt a SPIN® questioning style.

4 Plan, do and review

The majority of salespeople acknowledge the importance of call planning even if, in reality, their planning is no more than a few moments of anxiety before the call. However, only limited learning comes from planning the call, or from making it. The most important lessons come from the way you *review* the calls you make. After each call ask yourself such questions as:

- Did I achieve my objectives?
- If I were making that call again, what would I do differently?
- What have I learned that will influence future calls on this account?
- What have I learned that I can use elsewhere?

Unfortunately, few of us take enough time to ask ourselves systematically questions like these. Over the years I've had the opportunity to travel with dozens of the world's top salespeople. And, as a researcher, I've looked for any differences which mark them out from those who haven't made it to the top. Two differences stand out. The first is that top people I've travelled with put great emphasis on reviewing each call – dissecting what they've learned and thinking about possible improvement. The second difference is that most of the really successful sales-people I've studied recognise that their success depends on getting details right. They may have excellent skills in terms of broad, large-scale strategic account planning, but that's not what marks them out. Many of the less-successful people I've studied can give an impeccable account of themselves in terms of overall strategy. The difference that's so evident in top people is that they can translate into effective sales behaviour – they know what to *do* in the call. They understand detail, which may be why they put such emphasis on planning and reviewing each call.

It's worth asking yourself whether you are giving enough time to reviewing the detail of what happened in the call. Never be content with global conclusions like, 'it went quite well'. Ask yourself about the *details*. Did some parts of the call go better than others? Why? Which *specific* questions you asked had most influence on the customer? Which needs did the customer feel strongly? Which needs changed during the discussion? Why? Which of the behaviours you used had most impact? Unless you analyse your selling on this level of detail, you'll miss important opportunities for learning and improving your selling skills.

A final word

Perhaps the most significant conclusion I've come to from Huthwaite's research studies of selling is about the importance of detail. Many years ago, at the start of our research, I would have told you that sales success lay in the broader areas. I would have chosen global factors like personality, attitudes, interpersonal chemistry or overall account strategy to explain why one person sold better than another. I don't believe that any more. Increasingly our research has shown that success is constructed from those important little building-blocks called *behaviours*. It's the hundreds of minute behavioural details in a call which – more than anything else – will decide whether it succeeds.

I'm not the first to come to the conslusion that success rests on understanding the minute details. In 1801 William Blake wrote:

> He who would do good to another
> must do it in Minute Particulars.
> General Good is the plea of the scoun
> drel, hypocrite and flatterer;
> For Art and Science cannot exist but in
> minutely organised particulars.

So, as a parting word, let me urge you to concentrate on those minute particulars. Give real attention to the basic building-block behaviours you use when you sell. We've put thousands of sales calls under the microscope to isolate some of the detailed behavioural elements which bring success in the major sale. Use the results of our research to examine, develop and improve the minute particulars of your selling skills.

Appendix A

Evaluating the SPIN® models

More than a century ago Lord Kelvin wrote, 'if you cannot measure it – if you cannot express it in quantitative terms – then your knowledge is of a meagre and insignificant kind'. How right he was! But alas, today we live in an age which has lost the exuberance of the great nineteenth-century scientific investigators. Meaurement, proof and careful testing don't generate the same excitement as they did in the golden age of science. As a result our work on testing the validity of the SPIN® models gets relegated to an Appendix like this instead of being right in the middle of the book where Lord Kelvin would have put it.

If you're the one person in a hundred who bothers to read the Appendix in a book like this, then you deserve my admiration and gratitude. Personally, I find the material here to be the most exciting part of our work. I hope you'll find it rewarding too.

My topic is *proof*. How do we know that the methods I've described in the book really contribute to sales success? That's been the most difficult challenge in our research – collecting solid evidence that the models we've developed really bring a measurable improvement in bottom-line sales results. As far as I can tell, we're the first team to bring rigorous scientific methods to establishing whether particular selling skills result in measurable productivity improvement.

Many people, of course, have made *claims* that their models and methods bring dramatic improvements in sales results. As I look through my junk mail today there are several enticing promises of success. 'Double your sales' claims a one-day programme. 'At last' says another, 'a proven method which will increase your sales by up to 300 per cent'. A third offering tells me 'After this programme, the sales of our branch went through the roof. Yours will too!'. Yes, there's no shortage of *claims* made by training programmes that their methods bring measurable improvement. But how many of these dramatic cases stand up to close scrutiny? None that I've looked at. Unfortunately, when you examine them closely, most of the heavily advertised 'miracle cures' in sales training look remarkably similar to the claims made for snake oil a couple of hundred years ago.

I'm not being unduly malicious when I draw parallels between sales training and snake oil. Many of the purveyors of snake oil, miracle mixtures and wonder medicines sincerely believed that they had found a great cure. Their sincerity was based on a simple misperception. Put yourself in the shoes of an eighteenth-century country doctor. You're treating a very ill patient. You've tried everything, yet nothing seems to work. So, in desperation, you put together a mixture of herbs and potions. Your patient takes the mixture and recovers. Eureka! Your medicine works, you've found a miracle cure. What you don't see, in your enthusiasm, is that the patient was getting better anyway.

For the rest of your life you honestly believe it was your mixture which caused the recovery.

That's exactly what happens with most sales training. The designer puts together a mixture of concepts and models – and administers it in the form of a training programme. Afterwards there's an increase in sales so, in all sincerity, the training designer concludes that the training has *caused* the increase. I spent three years doing post-graduate research into training evaluation. Over and over again I'd come across this 'miracle cure' phenomenon. I recall, for example, a trainer from a large chemical company telling me that he had a programme which doubled sales. Sure enough, he had figures to prove his point – the sales of his division had risen by 118 per cent since the training. On looking closely at the curriculum, however, I found it was little different from the training which that division had been running for years. I couldn't find anything to justify a sudden 118 per cent increase in sales. But looking at the *market* told a different story. A large competitor had gone out of business because of industrial disputes, new products had been introduced, prices had changed. On top of that, there were several significant changes in sales force management and policy – not to mention a major advertising campaign. It's reasonable to suppose that each of these factors had a much larger impact on sales than a conventional sales training programme. In my judgement, the patient would have recovered without the miracle cure – the training was snake oil.

During my evaluation research I investigated many claims for sales increases resulting from training. More than 90 per cent of them could be accounted for more easily by other management or market factors. There are so many variables which affect sales performance – and training is just one factor. In almost every case we studied there was a more plausible reason for the increase. I'm not doubt-ing the sincerity of those who tell you how their wonderful sales method has doubled results. But, as with any miracle cure, you've got to ask whether the patient would have done equally well without the medicine.

Correlations and causes

Whether we're talking about medicine or training, it's extremely difficult to prove that your 'cure' is effective. Yet that's a difficulty I now face in this chapter, because the question I want to answer for you is, 'Does this method work?'. What's the evidence that the models we've put forward here will make a worthwhile contribution to your sales results? If you're going to invest time and effort in practising the sales skills I've described, you'll need to know that I'm offering you more than snake oil. But how can I *prove* to you that the SPIN® process increases sales?

Let me start with how *not* to do it. In the early days of the SPIN® model we were working with a capital goods company based just outside New York. The training staff were anxious to test whether the model brought improved sales results (see Figure A.1).

They measured the average monthly sales for the 28 people they trained. For the six months before training, the average sales were 3.1 orders per month. But, in the six months after the training, average sales rose to 4.9 orders a month – an increase of 58 per cent.

Can we conclude that the SPIN® model increases orders by 58 per cent? That would be a very unwise conclusion. Let's look more closely at the result. In the six months following the programme, two important new products were introduced. Sales territories were redrawn and 23 of the 28 trained people were given

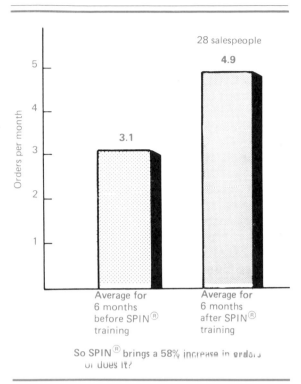

So SPIN® brings a 58% increase in orders or does it?

Figure A.1   A misleading example of improvement

larger territories with greater sales potential. Company sales increased during this time by approximately 35 per cent – and most of that increase came from *untrained* people. As we looked more closely, it became clear that we were in danger of kidding ourselves that SPIN® was a miracle cure when, in reality, we had no way to tell what part of the increase was due to SPIN® and what part resulted from other factors.

In the same vein, I have to advise you not to be taken in by this glowing little report of another SPIN® evaluation. This one is from Honeywell's *Management Magazine:*

Our European salesforce was oriented primarily to product and short cycle selling. We needed a truly effective programme . . . that could be applied universally to our varied European

markets. Late in 1978 the SPIN® programme was adapted into all European languages. There was a 20% increase in sales success . . . which may rise as the salesmen sharpen their SPIN® techniques.

Yes, following the implementation of the SPIN® approach there was a 20 per cent increase in sales. But what this report *doesn't* tell you is that Honeywell introduced a number of important new products to Europe that year, including the revolutionary TDC 2000 process control system. It's quite possible that the products created the whole increase. In Honeywell's case there's no way we can tell whether the SPIN® approach is any improvement on snake oil.

Control groups

The most serious weakness of results like these is that the trainers didn't set up a control group – a matched group of *untrained* people who could provide a baseline against which changes in the performance of the trained group could be judged. I imagine that the majority of readers will know about control groups and how important they are for any experimental work. But you may not know that much of the early use of control groups was in medicine, where they were used in an attempt to sort out whether a cure was genuine or just snake oil. If the trainers had set up a control group of 28 matched, untrained salespeople, we could have compared the performance of the two groups to obtain a truer picture.

But, even with a control group, results can be misleading. Here's a study which, on the surface, seems a very convincing test of whether the SPIN® model brings improved performance in major sales (see Figure A.2).

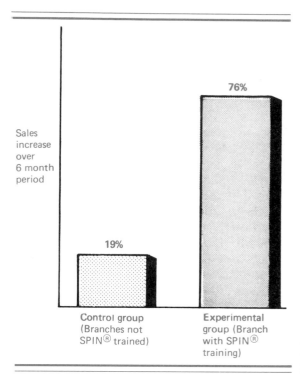

Figure A.2 A misleading control group study

The branch had been created very recently – just four months before the SPIN® training. The average selling cycle for the product range was three months. So the productivity improvement could well have been caused by the time required for a new branch to get up to speed, coupled with the delayed effects of a three-month sales cycle. Once again, our 'proof' can be explained away.

In our research files, we've many similar examples of evaluation studies which look plausible at a first glance, but don't stand up to close scrutiny. Here's one more case to make the point (Figure A.3). A large business machines company decided to evaluate the SPIN® methods in a seasonal market where February was a peak month.

In order to compensate for seasonal and market effects, they used as control groups every other branch which operated in the same market. The company tracked the order record of each branch before and after the experimental branch was trained in early January. As you can see, the SPIN® trained branch showed an impressive productivity gain compared with the others. This time, unlike our earlier studies, all five branches were well established – so there wasn't a problem about the selling cycle or the learning curve. Could this be the proof we'd been looking for? Unfortunately it wasn't.

In November the branch manager changed. How do we know whether the dramatic improvement in productivity was caused by the SPIN® models or by a new sales activity management system which he introduced in December? The question in unanswerable. Nevertheless, the company attempted an answer of sorts by interviewing all participating salespeople. They asked each person to estimate how much of the change was due to the SPIN® training and how much to other causes. Although everybody obligingly gave an estimate, the fact that their most common response was 50 per

In this case, a large multinational company decided to test the SPIN® model by training a whole major account branch of 31 salespeople. As a control they chose other branches which were not given the training. If the trained branch improved more than the others, then this wouldn't be due to the market or the products because those factors applied equally to both control and experimental branches. Even more important, there were no significant changes in people – the branch had unusually low turnover at both seller and manager levels. Perhaps, this time, we had a valid test of whether the SPIN® approach brings productivity.

The results, a 57 per cent gain compared with the control group, certainly look convincing. But we have to ask the standard evaluator's question, 'Is there any other equally plausible way to explain this increase?'. Unfortunately for us, there is.

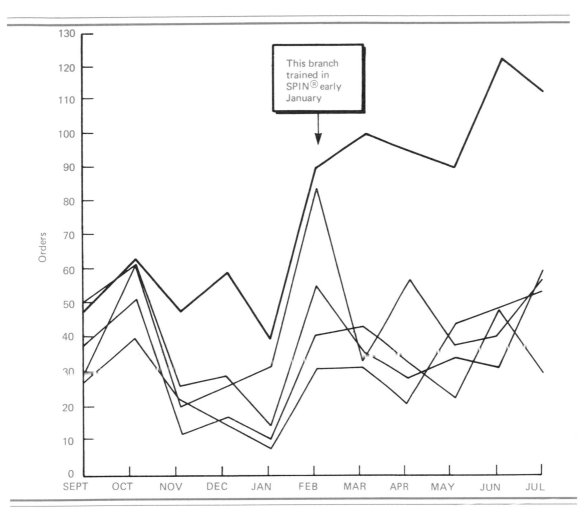

Figure A.3 Productivity gain of SPIN® trained branch compared with four control groups

cent was due to SPIN® makes me suspicious. Whenever somebody replies '50 per cent' to any question about causes, I interpret that as meaning that they haven't a clue.

Failure after failure

You can never entirely eliminate the effects of other organisational and market factors – which means that it's extremely difficult to obtain convincing proof of any selling model. Heaven knows, we've tried. We got one organisation to agree not to change products, management or salespeople for the whole of a six month test period. For a while we were convinced that we had an evaluation study which would stand up to the toughest scrutiny. Then, just as we were moving smoothly into the third month of the test, the wretched competition cut prices by 15 per cent. Our client, forced to respond quickly, changed prices, people and product introductions. Another test ruined!

We *thought* we finally had all important factors under control in a high-tech company. The test branch was doing well – 73

145

per cent ahead of the control branches – and this time we were convinced we had a winner. Half way through the test, however, we fell victim to one of the branch managers from the control group. Before the test, he'd been top branch and proud of it. But now, seeing that the test branch figures were looking much better than his own, he decided to take action. In the dead of night he raided the training department's files and made a copy of all programme materials which we'd used with the test branch. Returning home with his loot, he swore all his salespeople to secrecy and ran his own training classes using the stolen material.

It ruined our test. Although I was furious at the time, looking back I can't help thinking it's the most convincing evaluation study of all when your models are good enough for a sales manager to drive 600 miles in the middle of the night to steal them.

Is proof possible?

In 1970 I wrote a book on training evaluation with Peter Warr and Mike Bird. One of our conclusions was that the difficulties involved in controlling real-life variables made it impossible to prove that training increased productivity. While we were writing the book, we discussed an 'ideal' evaluation study. Mike Bird and I shared an office and we spent hours thinking about how we would set about designing the perfect piece of evaluation. Mike drew a picture on the blackboard (Figure A.4). 'If you look at it simply,' he said, 'the way most people set about evaluation is like this.'

'But', he added, 'look at all the complicating variables. How can you possibly prove whether any change is due to training?' He quickly sketched in some of the other factors (Figure A.5).

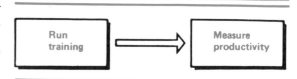

Figure A.4 Common approach to evaluation

This was turning into a depressing conversation, especially since I'd just been reading Karl Popper, the philosopher who's best known for claiming that you can't prove *anything*. What Popper had suggested is that the only way science can 'prove' something is by continually trying to *disprove* it and failing. 'Could we adopt that kind of approach?' I asked. 'Just suppose that instead of trying to prove training brings productivity, we attacked the problem from the other end and tried to *disprove* any productivity effect. Would that be better?'.

We didn't take the conversation further – but years later, as I wrestled with the problems of testing whether our SPIN® approach worked, I remembered that discussion with Mike. Should we forget about proof and instead set about *disproving* the idea that the skills described in this book cause more sales?

Proof or disproof – does it matter?

As a practical person, you may find my researcher's obsession with proof or disproof to be an academic form of overkill. In my defence I'd say that many billions of dollars are being wasted each year, teaching selling methods without one scrap of proof to show whether or not they work. No other area of business is so casual about testing its products or methods. Civilised society would collapse if manufacturing design showed the same lack of concern with product effectiveness that I see in most training design organ-

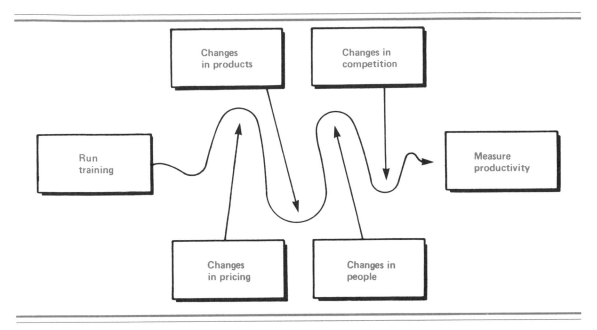

Figure A.5 Complicating variables in common approach to evaluation

isations. Just because it's difficult to measure the effectiveness of a sales approach doesn't mean we shouldn't try. On the contrary, the difficulties make it all the more important. Without honest attempts at better measurement of sales-training effectiveness, we'll continue to waste billions of dollars which could be spent more productively elsewhere. I don't really care whether the emphasis is on proof or disproof. But I *do* passionately support anything which will give better measurement and testing, because without those tests, my profession is in the snake oil business. If you'll forgive me a moment of preaching, I hope you'll see this concern with thorough evaluation as being in *your* interest. Our reason for all these measurements and tests is that we're trying to make sure that what we give you will work. There used to be an old army saying, 'if it moves, shoot it and if it doesn't move, paint it'. Huthwaite's equivalent is, 'if it moves, measure it and if you can't measure it, shoot it'. Measurement and testing is almost an obsession with us.

Stages of disproof

In pursuit of our enthusiasm for a rigorous measurement of the SPIN® approach, my Huthwaite colleagues and I spent unreasonable amounts of time struggling with the problems of proof and disproof. We decided that, before we looked at productivity gains, we first needed to pass two other tests – or opportunities for disproof as Popper would have called them.

Test 1   Do these skills make calls more successful?

How did we know we were teaching the right things? Before we could begin to answer elaborate questions about productivity change, we needed first to test whether the models worked. For example, suppose we were teaching a major account team a traditional low-value sales model which involved asking open and closed questions, giving advantages and then using closing techniques to gain commitment. From the evidence we've presented so far, it's not likely that adopting this model would make major account sales calls more successful. Even if there were substantial productivity gains after the training, they would probably have been caused by other factors. So, before we started to measure productivity gains, our first test had to establish whether we were teaching the right things.

Generically, we knew that the SPIN® models passed this test because they were derived from the studies of successful calls. So there was a high probability that if we taught the SPIN® skills, we would be teaching something which would make calls more successful. But if we wanted to design the ultimate evaluation study, we'd have to go beyond that. We'd have to answer a very *specific* question about the individual salespeople whose productivity we intended to measure. We couldn't rely on studies we'd done in other companies, in other markets or with other groups. What if this group was different? How did we know that just because SPIN® worked somewhere else, it would work here? In the ultimate evaluation test we would start by doing some research to establish what a successful call looks like *for the group of people we're going to train*. We couldn't take the chance that unique factors in terms of their geography, market, products or sales organisation might invalidate our results. If, from this first test, we could collect solid evidence that the things we were teaching worked for this set of individuals, that would have eliminated one more source of disproof (see Figure A.6).

Test 2   How do we know people are using the new skills?

The next test in our quest for disproof, would be to discover whether people were actually using the new skills in real calls after the training. I was once caught

out on this test. We were measuring productivity improvement in a group of salespeople from a division of General Electric. In the six months after the SPIN® based training, sales had risen by an average of 18 per cent. Could we claim the credit? Alas no. By watching these people sell before and after the training, we established that they weren't using significantly more of the SPIN® behaviours afterwards, than they were before we trained them. Once again we had disproved that the productivity gain should be credited to us.

This test, which measures whether the training has made people behave any differently in their calls, is rarely if ever carried out by training designers. It's a pity. We've learned a lot about effective training design by analysing the amount of behaviour change our programmes have caused. I'm sure that other designers would also find this kind of measurement more useful than the usual smiles test – 'the-training-must-be-good-because-people-say-they-liked-it' – which is the normal extent of training evaluation.

Bit by bit we were developing a specification for a very sophisticated and thorough method which we could use to evaluate the effectiveness of our SPIN® models. The evaluation steps would be:

- Watch a group of larger account salespeople in action to find whether there are more SPIN® behaviours used in their successful calls than in the calls which fail. If so, we've passed test 1 – we now know that the model works for this group of people.
- Train the group to use the SPIN® methods we are trying to evaluate.
- Go out with each person in the group after the training to discover whether they are now using more of the trained behaviours during their calls. If so, we've passed test 2 – we know that people are actually using the new skills.

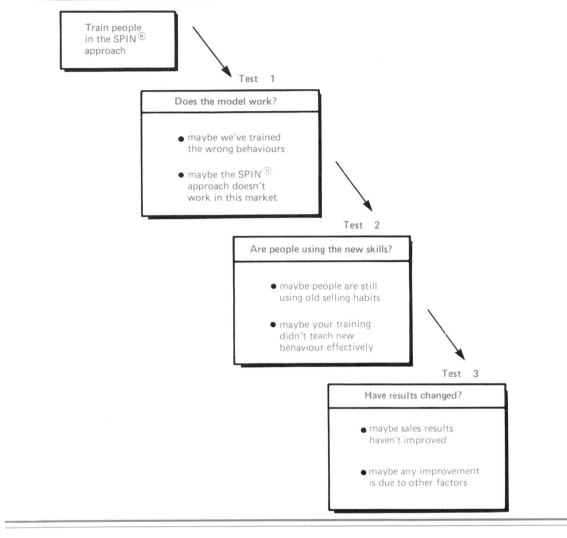

Figure A.6   Stages of proof or disproof

- Assuming that we pass on test 1 and test 2, measure productivity gain compared with control groups.

It seems an elaborate method, but we didn't see any alternative. We searched for a simpler answer but none of the usual superficial evaluation tests stood up to close examination. The author and corporate planning expert Michael Kami once told me, 'For every complex question there is a simple answer – and it is wrong'. We were forced to agree with him. If we wanted a solid evaluation of a complex problem, we'd have to accept a difficult method for getting there.

A test with Kodak – almost

We took our evaluation plan to a number of clients and tried to interest them in it. That's a polite way to say that we tried to get them to pay for a very expensive test. Most of them, realising how costly the test would be, encouraged us to take our evaluation elsewhere. For a time we had high hopes of a full test with Kodak – an organisation with a long tradition of careful testing of new methods. Kodak were considering using SPIN® based training worldwide across all their divisions involved in major sales. An evaluation test seemed a sensible first step. We agreed to test the model by observing a group of salespeople for their Health Sciences Division. Sure enough, the SPIN® model worked exactly as our research had predicted. Implication and need-payoff questions were more than twice as frequent in successful calls as in the ones which failed.

Next we trained the pilot group and, after the training, went out to observe whether they were using the new skills. Once again, things looked good. Benefits had trebled, implication questions had trebled, need-payoff questions had doubled. The group were now using more of the successful behaviours than they were before the training.

We were delighted. For the first time we were about to begin a productivity test where we could day, 'We *know* the model works and we *know* these people are using it in their calls'. Then came one of those good news, bad news bombshells. The good news was that Kodak were so happy with the pilot test that they had decided to adopt the SPIN® methods worldwide. The bad news was that they were so convinced by their people's reactions to the pilot that they didn't see any point in elaborate and costly productivity tests. The 'smiles test' had stabbed us in the back!

Enter Motorola Canada

We were just remarking to ourselves that the evaluator's lot was one of unrelieved woe, when we had an offer we couldn't refuse from Motorola. Like Kodak, they wanted to test the SPIN® model with the intention, if it worked, of adopting it

worldwide. Their chosen test group was the Communications Division of Motorola Canada. This time we were careful to set the evaluation study in concrete well before the project, so that none of our tests would escape. As an added bonus, Motorola hired an independent evaluator, Marti Bishop, who had worked with our models and methods in her previous job as Evaluation Manager in Xerox Corporation. Her function was to rigorously test the effectiveness of the SPIN® programme, going through the full steps we had outlined for the ideal productivity evaluation. I'm now quoting from a condensed version of her report:

Motorola Canada productivity study.

This report is a productivity analysis of the SPIN® programme that was conducted during the third quarter of 1981.

It sets out to answer these questions:

- Does the SPIN® model work in Motorola Canada?
- Are people using the model after the training?
- Has this led to measurable improvement in their productivity?

Does the model work?
Motorola's first concern is to test whether the SPIN® behaviours predict success in Motorola's sales calls in the way that they have proved successful in other companies.

To test this we travelled with each of the 42 sales reps who were to be trained and analysed the frequency of the SPIN® behaviours in their successful and unsuccessful calls.

We found that all behaviours were at a higher frequency in the successful calls:

	Successful calls
Situation questions	1% more
Problem questions	17% more*

Implication questions   53% more*
Need-payoff questions   60% more*
Benefits   64% more*
Features   5% more

* indicates item is statistically significant

The SPIN® training concentrated on developing an increased number of problem questions, implication questions, need-payoff questions and benefits. As each of these behaviours is at a significantly higher frequency in Motorola Canada's successful calls, we can conclude that the training is teaching people behaviours which should help them sell more effectively.

Have people changed?
There's evidence the model works in Motorola. The next step must be to show that the 42 people who were trained are actually using the new behaviours in their calls. To test this we observed people selling before the training period, during the training period and after it in order to determine whether they are now behaving differently with their customers. We sampled each of the 42 people at five points. The first time we went out with them was immediately before the training. The other four times were at intervals of approximately three weeks during the training period itself (see Figure A.7).

At the start of the training period people were asking more situation questions (average 8.6 per call) than the combined total of problem *plus* implication *plus* need-payoff questions (average 5.8 per call). So, the three questioning behaviours statistically associated with success were being used less than situation questions – the one questioning behaviour *not* significantly associated with success.

By the end of the training period, however, this had been reversed. The frequency of the successful questions had risen to 8.8 in the average call,

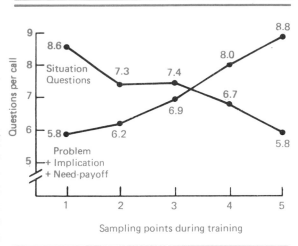

Figure A.7   Motorola Canada: changes in questioning behaviour

while the level of situation questions had fallen. In terms of questioning behaviour, we can safely conclude that the 42 salespeople are now behaving in a more successful way than before.

Benefits, at the start of the training, were at an average level of 1.2 per call (see Figure A.8).

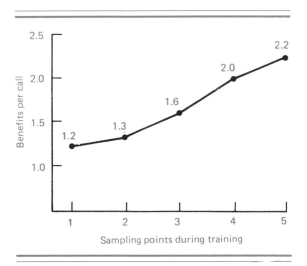

Figure A.8   Motorola Canada: changes in benefits per call

151

By the end of the training, benefits have risen to 2.2 per call. Remember that benefits, of all behaviours, are the ones most predictive of success in Motorola Canada calls. Your salespeople are now giving customers almost twice as many benefits per call as they were before the training. In view of this, it would not be surprising if this pilot results in measurable sales increases.

Has productivity changed?
To measure productivity change I have:

● Examined the sales results for the 42 people in the pilot and compared them with a control group of 42 untrained salespeople from Motorola Canada.

● Compared results for three time periods:

three months *before* the SPIN® training

three months *during* the SPIN® implementation period

three months *after* the implementation

The results therefore span a nine month period.

● Measured sales in terms of:
total orders
orders from existing accounts
orders from new accounts
dollar value of sales.
Figure A.9 shows the changes in total order levels.

In terms of total orders, the 42 people in the control group have shown a 13 per cent fall from their original pre-training level. This is due to the competitiveness of the communications marketplace, coupled with the extremely difficult Canadian economy. In contrast, the SPIN® trained group has shown a 17 per cent gain, reversing the trends of a difficult market. This gross difference between control and experiment group of 30 per cent in order rate is statistically significant.

The management of Motorola Canada was focusing its effort on increasing new business and wanted to know whether the SPIN® training made a significant contribution to new business sales (Figure A.10).

As you can see, new business sales for

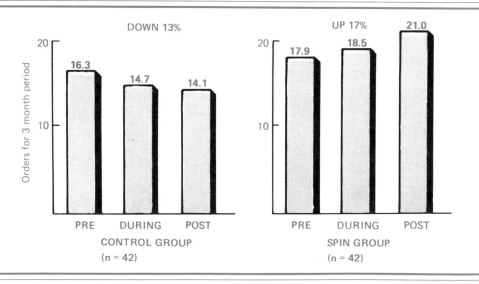

Figure A.9 Motorola Canada: changes in total order levels

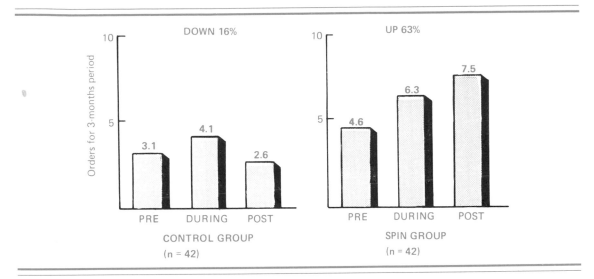

Figure A.10   Motorola Canada: changes in new business orders

the control group show an increase only during the training period, when the sales organisation was putting great effort into new business sales. However, in the period after training, sales fell back to below their original level, reflecting the difficulties in the market.

In contrast, the SPIN® trained group showed an order gain of 63 per cent, reversing the generally poor market performance. It's particularly interesting to note the increase in the SPIN® trained group's orders in the period *after* the training had ended. This suggests that the new skills are now self-maintaining and can be expected to make a continued impact on sales productivity. Before the study some of your sales managers had expressed reservations about the 'soft' nature of the SPIN® model, with its emphasis on probing and not on the 'hard' closing techniques which some managers felt to be essential to the new business sale in a very difficult and competitive market. From these results it would seem that they have no reason to be worried. The SPIN® training has succeeded in generating significant business against hard-sell competition.

In terms of business generated from existing accounts, the record of the control group is better (Figure A.11).

Both groups show a fall in business from existing accounts during the training. This is due to the sales organisation's focus on new business during that period. However, while the control group shows a 13 per cent overall decline, the SPIN® trained group shows a 1 per cent increase.

An increase in orders can be misleading. It's possible that the productivity gain of the SPIN® group was because they took more small orders, while the control group took fewer orders but each one had a greater dollar value. Because of this possibility, we also need to take a direct measure of the dollar value of sales. Dollar sales figures are confidential and this is a report for general release. We have therefore displayed the change in dollar value for the two groups in percentage terms to preserve confidentiality (Figure A.12).

The control group showed a decline of 22.1 per cent in terms of dollars sold. Again, this reflects the extraordinarily

153

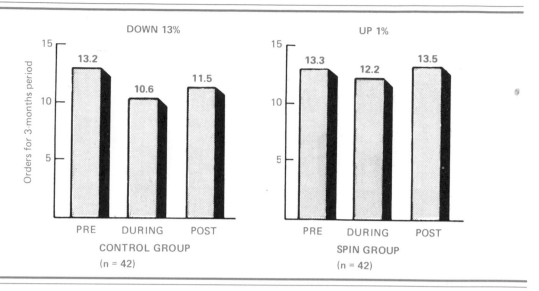

DOWN 13%

UP 1%

CONTROL GROUP
(n = 42)

SPIN GROUP
(n = 42)

Figure A.11   Motorola Canada: changes in orders from existing customers

difficult market conditions. The SPIN® trained group reversed this trend, showing an overall gain of 5.3 per cent in dollar value. Note that these results suggest that some of the dramatic 63 per cent order increase made by the SPIN® group in the new business area

does come from a larger number of smaller orders.

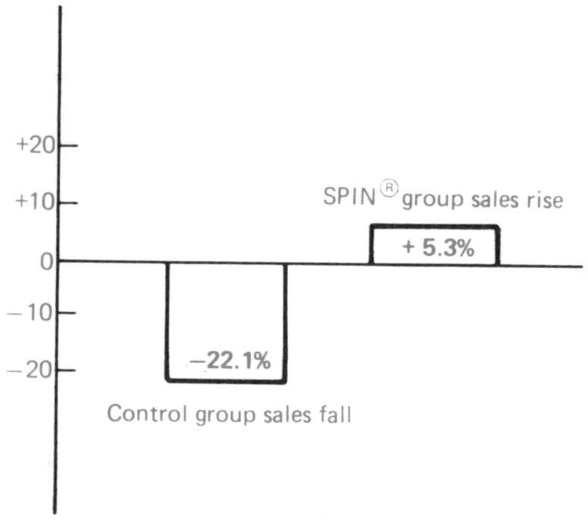

In terms of dollar sales, the SPIN® group is running at 27.4 per cent above the control group. This difference is substantial and statistically significant. It would seem that the cost and effort of implementing the SPIN® approach has been repaid many times over in terms of sales results.

Conclusions

These results suggest that the SPIN® approach has succeeded in:
● changing the skill levels of the people trained
● increasing order levels, particularly in the new business area
● increasing the dollar volume of sales by an average of 27 per cent above the control group.

+20

+10

0

−10

−20

SPIN®group sales rise

+ 5.3%

−22.1%

Control group sales fall

Figure A.12   Motorola Canada: pre/post change in dollar value of sales

Two serious flaws

Marti Bishop's evaluation study represented the most detailed, rigorous and comprehensive examination of a sales training programme ever carried out. I've quoted here from the summary version, but that's just the tip of the iceberg. She used additional control groups, methodologies which involved sales managers in the data collection process and some sophisticated computer techniques to build success models and analyse results. If you're interested in such things, you'll find further details at the end of this appendix. But, powerful though this study is, it still doesn't contain that elusive 'proof' which we were looking for.

If I wanted to discredit the Motorola study, I'd point out two flaws each of which could be potentially serious enough to give a strict methodologist palpitations.

- The control group starts from a lower point than the SPIN® group. If you look at order levels before training, the control group averaged 16.3 orders and the SPIN® group 17.9. Now this difference isn't statistically significant, so perhaps it's nothing to worry about. Nevertheless, a cynic might argue that the SPIN® group did better in a difficult economy because they were a little better to begin with.
- There might be a 'Hawthorne effect'. That's a technical term for the artificial increase in results which you get from paying attention to people. The name comes from the Hawthorne plant of Western Electric where, in the late 1920s some of the early productivity studies were carried out. In one of the Hawthorne experiments researchers found that when they increased the intensity of the plant's lighting, productivity rose. But, to their astonishment, productivity also rose when they *decreased* the lighting levels. Their conclusion was that you can get a short-term increase in productivity just by giving people attention. In the Motorola study, you could argue, the

productivity increase came from all the training attention which the SPIN® group were receiving. It wouldn't matter whether we trained the group in the SPIN® methods or in aerobic dancing. Productivity would have risen anyway because of the Hawthorne effect.

I had a couple of standard answers prepared to counter any suggestion that the change was due to a Hawthorne effect. My first defence was that Hawthorne effects are much less common than most people suppose and, when they do occur, they are short-term – usually lasting for a matter of days at the most. The Motorola study, which spanned a nine-month evaluation period would almost certainly be free of any serious Hawthorne effect. My second defence was, 'Who cares? The fact is that we've increased productivity. If it's a Hawthorne effect, then let's Hawthorne the whole sales force and get a 30 per cent increase in sales from everybody'. But my heart wasn't in either of these answers. The researcher in me badly wanted to know whether a Hawthorne effect existed and, if so, how much it had contributed to the productivity gain.

A new evaluation test

Motorola was convinced enough by the study to adopt the SPIN® methods worldwide. Because they were satisfied it worked, they saw no value in further attempts to *disprove* the link between SPIN® and productivity. In fact, they dismissed my concern as an example of that rather quaint eccentricity which the English show in times of stress. We needed a new client with enough doubt to justify another large-scale investigation. Salvation came in the form of a giant multinational business machines company who, like Motorola, wished to test

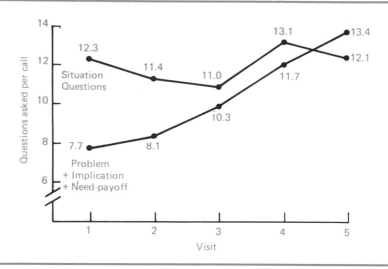

Figure A.13   Changes in questioning behaviour

SPIN® for worldwide application. With only moderate difficulty, I persuaded them to let me carry out the remaining two tests which would plug the gaps in the Motorola study.

First, we went through the same methodology which we had used in Motorola. I'll spare you the detailed findings, which were very similar to those in Motorola except that:

● Situation questions were 4 per cent *lower* in successful calls. This is consistent with our main research findings, where situation questions had a slightly negative effect on customers.

● As in Motorola, problem, implication and need-payoff questions were all significantly higher in successful calls. So were benefits. But unlike Motorola, where need-payoff questions were the most strongly associated with success, the most powerful behaviour in this study turned out to be implication questions.

Behaviour change brought about by the training was greater in this implementation than in Motorola (see Figure A.13).

In this case, problem, implication and need-payoff questions almost doubled, while the level of situation questions remained fairly constant.

Benefits showed a particularly pleasing rise – from 1.1 per call to 3.4 (see Figure A.14). That may not sound much but here's how I looked at it. The 55 people

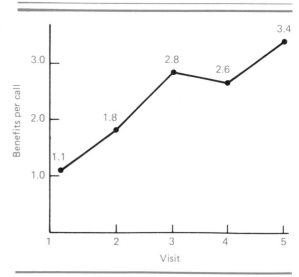

Figure A.14   Changes in benefits

trained in the study were making an average of 16 sales a week. That means, in an average week before the SPIN® training, there were 968 benefits offered to customers. At the end of the study, in an average week the same people were giving 2992 benefits. It would be surprising *not* to get a significant increase in sales from those 2000 extra benefits.

A matched control group

In this study we had an opportunity to match the control group so that both groups started with the same order level. This allowed us to test one possible weakness in our Motorola results – that the reason for the increase could be because the SPIN® group started from a higher point (see Figure A.15).

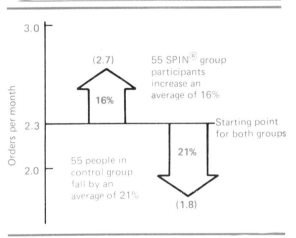

Figure A.15 Changes in productivity after training

Again, as in Motorola, we compared the performance of each group for a three-month *pre* and a three-month *post* period. The matched control group showed a 21 per cent fall in orders, while the SPIN® group showed a 16 per cent gain. This study was also carried out under unfavourable economic and competitive

conditions, which accounts for the fall in control group orders.

By matching the initial order levels of the control group in this way, we can confidently reject the idea that the reason for Motorola's 30 per cent gain in productivity was that the SPIN® group were better salespeople to begin with. That explanation can't be true here, where initial order levels of both groups are the same.

Measuring the Hawthorne effect

The Hawthorne effect was harder to test. As far as we know, nobody before us had ever tried to measure whether a Hawthorne element existed in sales training. As we thought about the problem, it became easy to see why we were the first. It's not hard to measure the impact of plant lighting on output, but how do you measure whether sales productivity gain is due to the SPIN® model or just because you've given attention to people by offering them training?

The method we adopted was a little complex, but that's inevitable given the difficulty of the issue we were trying to measure. Basically, the approach we used was this:

- We reanalysed the productivity results from our group of 55 people trained to use the SPIN® approach. Each of these people had exactly the same number of hours of training, so all 55 had received a similar level of attention. All had, so to speak, an identical dose of the Hawthorne effect.
- We divided our 55 people into two sub-groups. In any other group, learning any skill – whether it's golf, a foreign language or selling – some people naturally learn more than others. In one group, we put half of the 55 people who, from our measurement of their behaviour in calls, were

displaying the most use of the SPIN® behaviours. In the other group, we put the rest of the people, whose use of the SPIN® behaviours was much lower.

- We compared the sales results of the two groups. If productivity gain was entirely due to a Hawthorne effect, then both groups should show identical gain, because both groups had received the same amount of training and management attention. But, if productivity gain was due to using the SPIN® models, then the group showing the greatest learning of SPIN® should have much higher productivity gain than the group showing a poorer level of learning.
- Finally, we compared the performance of both groups with a similar

sized control group to make sure that the changes weren't caused by a market, product or organisational effect.

Once we'd decided on this methodology, we set about a re-examination of our data in an attempt to isolate the elusive Hawthorne effect (Figure A.16).

Our results showed that there *was* a Hawthorne effect at work but – as with most Hawthorne effects – its impact was short-lived.

First, let's look at the performance of the group higher on SPIN® skills. Their results show an increase *during* the training period, when they were receiving most attention. But, more important, their results continue to improve *after* the train-

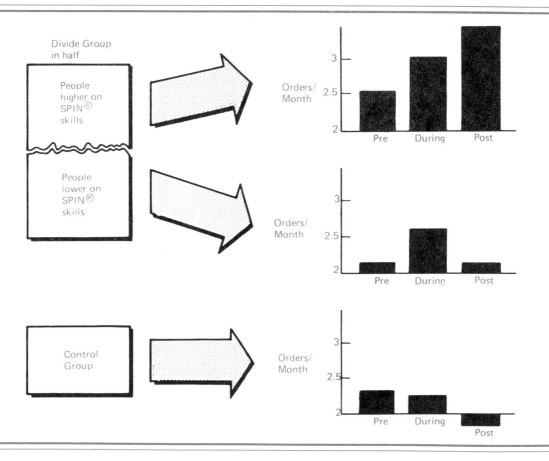

Figure A.16   Isolating the Hawthorne effect

ing is over, when they are receiving no attention which might create a Hawthorne effect.

In contrast, the results from the group lower on SPIN® skills shows a dramatic improvement *during* the four month training period. However, as soon as the training attention is withdrawn, their results slip back to the original level. Here we have the Hawthorne effect – isolated for the first time in the field of sales performance.

Finally, let's look at the control group. Selling the same products, in the same difficult capital goods market, their performance shows a decrease both during and after the training. So we can conclude that the improvement of the higher SPIN® group isn't because of market or product factors. Compared with the control group, even the performance of the lower SPIN® group looks good. Instead of a gradual decline, they are at least holding their own.

Final thoughts on evaluation

There are even more tests I'd like to carry out before I'll be totally satisfied that the models I've described in this book will significantly improve the results of major sales. It's a never ending quest. When I was growing up in Borneo there were no roads and all trips were by river. At any point of any journey, if you asked the boatman how much further, you'd get the same reply, *'Satu tanjong lagi'*, – which means, 'one more bend'. Evaluation studies are like that. Just when you think you've all the proof you need, there's one more bend.

We'll probably never get round that final bend. But, in our search for proof, I hope you'll agree that Huthwaite has explored the river carefully. We've tried to take an objective and critical look at our own models and whether they work – and, by doing so, we've become better researchers, designers and trainers. Above all, we've been able to increase the practical effectiveness of our approach. Ironically, by going through these very academic-sounding testing routines, we've improved our understanding of what makes practical good sense, measured by its contribution to sales results. I wish more people in the training business could be persuaded to take a similar approach. It would be very satisfying to us if this book stimulated more research into effective selling. I'd like to think that eventually, through patient investigation and experiment, researchers will be able to take more of the mystery out of the major sale and make it as clearly understandable as any other business function.

Technical talk

I've written this book for practising salespeople and their managers. Consequently I've said relatively little about technical points such as methodology, research procedures and statistical tests. For those specialists – academics, trainers, researchers, marketing experts and the like – who have technical questions, here are a few notes on our procedures.

A   Methodology

1   Observation as a method

Quantitative, frequency-based observational methodologies are little used in academic studies, partly because of their high cost and partly because observation-based methods take too much time in a publish or perish environment. There are also technical issues of inter-rater reliability. In our procedures it has taken us between three days and two weeks – depending on the complexity of the data collection instruments – to train observers to a criterion accuracy of r = 0.9. Further details of the method, its development and some of the issues involved in building behaviour-analysis instruments can be found in *Behaviour Analysis in Training*, Rackham & Morgan, McGraw Hill (1977).

2 Successful performers versus successful calls

The first methodological decision in observation studies is to establish a criterion for success by which the interaction under investigation can be evaluated. In many of our early studies, our criterion was the track record of the individual we were observing. We compared the behaviour of very successful salespeople with the behaviour of those salespeople whose track record was poor or average. Increasingly we've moved away from this outcome criterion because:

● The halo effect is hard to control if observers know that they are watching a good performer.

● Intervening market variables such as territory and account size can give a less-skilled person a good track record or, conversely, can mean that a skilled person may have a poorer record.

● Using the individual as the criterion brings interpersonal contaminants such as the salespeople's energy and activity levels.

Sales interactions are delightful for the researcher because each call has a classifiable outcome (order, advance, continuation, or no-sale). In our studies of management and supervisory interaction, setting such clear outcome criteria has been more difficult. In our experience, criteria which are based on the outcome of individual calls have provided us with clearer data than criteria based on overall track record.

3 Association and causes

We've convincingly shown, from dozens of studies at the 1 per cent probability level and beyond, that the behaviours we've described here are *associated* with success – that they occur at a higher frequency in calls leading to orders and advances. But a correlation doesn't mean a cause. There's a high correlation between the incidence of venereal disease in the port of Liverpool during the nineteenth century and the level of iron ore imports, yet nobody suggests that iron ore *causes* venereal disease. Are we guilty of specious reasoning – suggesting that because the SPIN® behaviours are correlated with successful calls, they are *causing* success? The only valid test of cause would be to teach the behaviours to a group of people not presently using them and to measure changes in their sales performance. It's for this reason that we carried out most of the evaluation studies reported in chapter 11. Other ways of detecting probable causal relationships which we've used included sequence analysis of seller and customer behaviour.

B Procedures

---

1 Categories per instrument

In total we studied 116 different sales behaviours. Inter-rater reliability becomes an increasing problem as the number of categories in any observation instrument increases. We therefore generally restricted individual instruments to a maximum of 20 behaviours.

2 Standardisation

Initial category definition was carried out by case discussion between central Huthwaite Research Group team members. The next iteration involved analysis of transcript material and listing of boundary examples between confusable categories. From there we prepared standard audiotapes, teaching transcripts and boundary exercises to use as test material in the training of observers. Observer reliability was developed by real time and transcript categorisation of many hundreds of sales behaviours examples. For criterion test of reliability we prepared standardised test tapes and used rank order correlation techniques across the category totals for the instrument being trained. Individual research projects frequently involved an extended period of observational work. Sometimes we had as many as 40 observers collecting data over a five-month period. In order to obtain observation standardisation over time, our normal procedure was to have monthly meetings with the observers where we gave reliability tests, coupled with periodic blind categorisation of standard audiotapes sent to observers by mail. No standardisation can be perfect, but we believe we maintained a level of reliability considerably higher than is customary in observation work of this kind.

C Statistics

Working with inherently noisy data the inevitable temptation is to use factor analytic methods. It's a temptation we avoided. During pilot work with any category system we initially used non-parametric tests. Although less-powerful than the classic parametric equivalents, our judgment was that the data we were dealing with failed to meet normality assumptions and that – in most cases – non-parametrics would be more conservative. The exception was when sample size grew very large. Non-parametric tests become increasingly cumbersome as sample numbers grow. What's more, the normality assumptions in the sample be-

come more acceptable with large samples. Whenever we report significance in this book:

- significance level is minimally 0.05.
- when the group of calls being tested numbers 59 or less we have normally used the Mann Whitney U test.
- when the group of calls numbers 60 or more we have used 't' tests.
- in those studies where we made directional predictions of outcome, we've used one-tailed significance level tests.

Cluster analyses, particularly McQuitty linkages, have proved particularly useful in helping us identify and redefine highly correlated categories. Personally, I like simple tests where there's immediate and visible indication of what's happening within the data matrix. It's for that reason we've avoided the arcane mysteries of factor analytic methods.

D Comments

Very complex sales have behavioural, tactical and strategic elements interacting in a way which is too complex to deal with in a book of this sort. I've concentrated here on the behavioural elements because we feel that those are the least understood and the worst trained. The models I've described in this book are particularly predictive in the early stages of the selling cycle. Much of our current research concentrates on the skills and strategies which predict success in later parts of the cycle.

Appendix B

Closing attitude scale

In chapter ten, we looked at closing techniques and I mentioned an attitude scale which we developed to measure people's feelings about closing. If you'd like to test yourself, then:

- read the 15 statements about closing
- after each statement, put a tick in the box which most nearly represents your own opinion
- follow the instructions at the end of the scale to calculate and interpret your score.

1 *Closing is the most valuable of all techniques for increasing sales.*

5 ☐ strongly agree

4 ☐ agree

3 ☐ uncertain

2 ☐ disagree

1 ☐ strongly disagree

2 *Trying to close a sale too often will reduce your chances of success.*

1 ☐ strongly agree

2 ☐ agree

3 ☐ uncertain

4 ☐ disagree

5 ☐ strongly disagree

3 *Unless you know a lot of closing techniques, you will be unable to sell effectively.*

5 ☐ strongly agree

4 ☐ agree

3 ☐ uncertain

2 ☐ disagree

1 ☐ strongly disagree

4 *Even at the start of a sale it never hurts to use a trial close.*

5 ☐ strongly agree

4 ☐ agree

3 ☐ uncertain

2 ☐ disagree

1 ☐ strongly disagree

5   *Weak closing is the most common cause of lost sales.*

    1 ☐ strongly agree

    2 ☐ agree

    3 ☐ uncertain

    4 ☐ disagree

    5 ☐ strongly disagree

6   *Customers are less likely to buy if they recognise that you are using closing techniques.*

    1 ☐ strongly agree

    2 ☐ agree

    3 ☐ uncertain

    4 ☐ disagree

    5 ☐ strongly disagree

7   *You cannot close too often when selling.*

    5 ☐ strongly agree

    4 ☐ agree

    3 ☐ uncertain

    2 ☐ disagree

    1 ☐ strongly disagree

8   *Closing techniques don't work with professional buyers.*

    1 ☐ strongly agree

    2 ☐ agree

    3 ☐ uncertain

    4 ☐ disagree

    5 ☐ strongly disagree

9   *The ABC of selling is Always Be Closing.*

    5 ☐ strongly agree

    4 ☐ agree

    3 ☐ uncertain

    2 ☐ disagree

    1 ☐ strongly disagree

10 *It's your other behaviour earlier in the sale, not your closing technique, which determines whether a customer will buy.*

    1 ☐ strongly agree

    2 ☐ agree

    3 ☐ uncertain

    4 ☐ disagree

    5 ☐ strongly disagree

11 *You should try to close every time that you see a buying signal.*

    5 ☐ strongly agree

    4 ☐ agree

    3 ☐ uncertain

    2 ☐ disagree

    1 ☐ strongly disagree

12 *From the moment you enter the customer's office, you should act as though the sale has already been made.*

5 ☐ strongly agree

4 ☐ agree

3 ☐ uncertain

2 ☐ disagree

1 ☐ strongly disagree

13 *If the customer resists your trial close, then it's a sign that you should have closed more forcefully.*

5 ☐ strongly agree

4 ☐ agree

3 ☐ uncertain

2 ☐ disagree

1 ☐ strongly disagree

14 *No matter how good your other skills, unless you have good closing techniques you will never succeed.*

5 ☐ strongly agree

4 ☐ agree

3 ☐ uncertain

2 ☐ disagree

1 ☐ strongly disagree

15 *Using closing techniques early in the sale is a sure way to antagonise customers.*

1 ☐ strongly agree

2 ☐ agree

3 ☐ uncertain

4 ☐ disagree

5 ☐ strongly disagree

How to calculate your score

You can calculate your score by taking the number, between 1 and 5 for each item, and totalling it across all 15 items.

Theoretically, a score of 45 is absolutely neutral. A higher score shows a positive attitude to closing and a lower score a negative attitude. In practice, most salespeople score a little above 45, and in our studies we allowed for this by taking a score of above 50 as demonstrating a favourable attitude to closing.

What do the scores mean?

In the study described in chapter 10, salespeople with the best results were those with a low (unfavourable) score, of less than 50.

But, as chapter 10 explains, the effectiveness of closing techniques depends on the type of sale. If your experience is with:

● low value goods and services
● unsophisticated customers
● no after-sale relationship with the customer

then a very favourable (above 50) attitude to closing might well be justified in terms of your selling situation. But if you score above 50 on this test and your business involves larger sales, sophisticated customers and a continuing post-sale relationship, please read chapter 10 very carefully. In the larger sale, closing techniques are more of a liability than an asset.

Index